FIVE ARTISTS
OF THE OLD WEST

"Free Trappers," painting by Charles M. Russell

Historical Society of Montana

FIVE ARTISTS
OF
THE OLD WEST

BY CLIDE HOLLMANN

~~~~~~

GEORGE CATLIN · KARL BODMER

ALFRED JACOB MILLER · CHARLES M. RUSSELL

FREDERIC REMINGTON

With Reproductions of the Artists' Paintings

~~~~~~

HASTINGS HOUSE · *Publishers* New York

CONTENTS

LIST OF ILLUSTRATIONS

AND PERMISSIONS

7

Moennitarri Warrior in Dog Dance. *Joslyn Art Museum, Omaha, Nebraska.*
Indian Utensils and Arms. *Joslyn Art Museum, Omaha, Nebraska.*
Indians Hunting the Bison. *Joslyn Art Museum, Omaha, Nebraska.*

ALFRED JACOB MILLER

Pierre and the Buffalo. *Walters Art Gallery, Baltimore, Maryland.*
Indians Watching the Caravans. *Walters Art Gallery, Baltimore, Maryland.*
Campfire – Preparing the Evening Meal. *Walters Art Gallery, Baltimore, Maryland.*
Laramie's Fort. *Walters Art Gallery, Baltimore, Maryland.*

FREDERIC REMINGTON

The Bronco Buster. (Bronze) *Museum of Art, University of Kansas, Lawrence, Kansas.*
Stampeding the Wagon Train Horses. *Museum of Art, University of Kansas, Lawrence, Kansas.*
The Scout. *Nelson-Atkins Gallery, Kansas City, Missouri.*
The Cavalryman. *Nelson-Atkins Gallery, Kansas City, Missouri.*
Fired On. *Smithsonian Institution, Washington, D.C.*

CHARLES M. RUSSELL

Jerk Line. *C. M. Russell Gallery, Great Falls, Montana.*
Indian Camp. *C. M. Russell Gallery, Great Falls, Montana.*
Fireboat. *C. M. Russell Gallery, Great Falls, Montana.*
The Thoroughman's Home on the Range. *C. M. Russell Gallery, Great Falls, Montana.*
Four Generations. *C. M. Russell Gallery, Great Falls, Montana.*

INTRODUCTION

INDIAN PICTOGRAPHS

THE EARLIEST ARTISTS of the Old West or of any part of America were, of course, the Indians. To appreciate the history of western art, including the work of the five men whose lives and paintings are described in this book, it is helpful to know something about that early Indian work, in the form of pictographs.

Since the Western Indians had no written language they made pictographs to keep records of tribal matters.

A pictograph was an arrangement of lines — straight, curved, or wavy; triangles, squares, circles, flat figures and other symbols, each representing some person, event or idea. Some were ingeniously outlined in color but all were stylized, somewhat like the hieroglyphics of ancient Egypt. Each symbol told a story.

Perhaps the best-known Indian pictograph (to the white people) was the Dakotah Calendar or "Winter Count" made by Lone Dog and covering the years 1799-1879. Each symbol, chosen by Lone Dog, the official chronicler, represented an incident of special significance that occurred during the year.

9

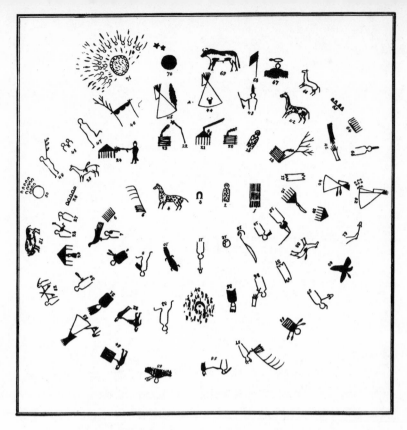

Lone Dog's Dakotah Calendar or Winter Count
Covering the years 1799-1870*

Symbol No. 1, in the center of the buffalo robe on which
the count was marked, consists of thirty straight perpendicular
lines in groups of three and tells that thirty Dakotas were
killed (1799). No. 2, a small figure covered with dots, tells
that smallpox broke out in the Dakota nation. No. 3, a horse-
shoe print, says that Dakotas had found a horse with shoes on.
No. 10 notes that Chief Little Beaver set fire to a trading store
and was killed.

Further entries included: No. 22, a meteor or comet was
seen. No. 17, buffalo meat was plentiful. No. 18, a Canadian
built a trading store with dry timber. No. 42, thirty spotted
ponies were stolen by Feather-in-the-Ear. No. 57, Four Horn
was appointed a medicine man.

* Each symbol chosen by Lone Dog, the official chronicler, represents an incident of special significance that occurred during the year.

1

EARLY WESTERN PAINTERS

THE LIST OF ARTISTS who painted the old west is a long and distinguished one. This book deals with three early artists and two later ones, who comprise the top five "picture writers" of the primitive West: George Catlin, Karl Bodmer, Alfred Jacob Miller, Frederic Remington and Charles M. Russell.

The Indians named the artists "picture writers" but some of them were writers in the more literal sense. George Catlin wrote long and accurate notes about every portrait and sketch. He also published several books containing his pictures and folios of prints.

Bodmer illustrated the books published by his patron, Prince Maximilian of Weid-Neuweid, Rhenish Prussia. Bodmer was also an etcher and did wood-block engravings.

Alfred Jacob Miller did most of his storytelling in his wonderful water colors, but he was an avid and entertaining letter writer.

11

Frederic Remington, in addition to his dramatic and stirring sketches, wrote books, articles for journals and short stories which he illustrated; he also acted as a war-correspondent in the Spanish-American war.

Charles M. Russell wrote books about the northwest country as he knew it and illustrated them with priceless paintings of rugged action.

2

George Catlin, 1796-1872
FIRST IN THE WEST

GEORGE CATLIN STUDIED LAW like other sons of the educated
men of his day. As a young lawyer, however, he spent less
time in the courtroom than at Peale's Museum in Independence
Hall in Philadelphia. When he *was* in court, he did more
sketching of the people who came to watch the process of
law and justice than he did arguing cases. At the age of
twenty-four he took down his lawyer's sign and put up one
that read "George Catlin, Painter of Miniatures." The following year he exhibited some of his work at the Pennsylvania
Art Academy. Painting miniatures, a popular art form of the
day, brought Catlin considerable fame and also a good amount
of money, but the small portraits did not satisfy his urge to
paint. He still was not doing the thing he most wanted to do.

George's friend, Charles Wilson Peale, was a famous portrait painter and self-trained taxidermist. In his museum he
had a collection of Indian relics as well as specimens of natural
history. Here Catlin spent a great deal of time. One day when
he was looking at the relics brought back by the famous
Lewis and Clark expedition of 1804-1805, he had a strong

desire to learn more about Indians and to help their cause.

Several of Peale's portraits of Indians hung on the walls. George glanced away from his study of them to see a group of chiefs of the Plains tribes, who had been brought East to visit the Great White Father in Washington, enter at the open door of the Museum. It seemed to the young artist that the portraits had come alive. The chiefs, in their elaborately trimmed costumes, made such a fine show that George immediately decided to go West where he could see and paint Indians in their native surroundings.

Just making up his mind to go West was easy, but he also had to earn the money to pay the expenses of the trip. So George began to speed up his output of portraits. His work had become so popular that he could have had a fine career in that field like that of his friend Peale.

During this period Catlin was very busy with commissions to paint wealthy and distinguished men, but he found time to make trips to the Indian reservations of western New York. There he painted some of the natives, including the famous Red Jacket of the Seneca tribe. These were not the wild and picturesque red men he had dreamed of putting on canvas but he made careful sketches and later showed them to General Clark in support of his request to be allowed to travel into the primitive West.

George Catlin was a handsome, wiry man of medium height with dark skin and hair and intensely blue eyes. He was socially acceptable in spite of his odd ideas about championing the cause of the Indians. He made friends in high places as well as among the savages. It was at a party in the governor's mansion at Albany, New York, that he met beautiful, dark-haired Clara Gregory, daughter of a wealthy Albany family, and fell in love.

They were married in Albany on May 10, 1828, when the

War Dance, Teton, Dekota *George Catlin*

artist was thirty-two years old and his bride just twenty. Clara knew that he was set on going west to paint the Plains Indians and encouraged him in this ambition. However, when the time came to start, she was ill of a fever and had to be left behind with the elder members of the Catlin family.

These included George's father, Putnam Catlin, who had enlisted in the Revolutionary Army at age thirteen and served as regimental fife-major in the Second Connecticut Regiment. George's grandfather, Eli Catlin, had been a Revolutionary Army lieutenant. Perhaps the fact that George came from such stalwart forebears helped to sustain him later in the rugged life among the savages of the early West.

He also had a brave inheritance from his mother, Polly

Sutton Catlin. In 1797 when Putnam Catlin moved his family from Wilkes-Barre, Pennsylvania, to a farm forty miles from the town, stout-hearted Polly rode horseback through the woods to their new home on the Susquehanna River, carrying her infant son, George, in her arms.

Along with the pioneer strength of this family went a cultured home life. George and the thirteen other Catlin children — four older and nine younger — grew up in an atmosphere of good books and gentle manners. So when George left his wife at home in Pennsylvania and took a packet boat to St. Louis (the starting-place for all western travel at that time) he knew she would receive tender care.

George himself was in good hands. General William Clark was then superintendent of Indian affairs, with authority over travel among the Indians. From him the young artist received permission to make himself at home in the general's office in St. Louis, and to paint the Indians who came there.

This was the General Clark who, as Captain William Clark, had made the great western expedition with Captain Meriwether Lewis. It was the Indian relics and trappings from this expedition that Catlin had often studied in Peale's Museum, back in Philadelphia. Now the general, still strong and active, had his own collection of Indian relics in St. Louis. With them were many crude pictures by James Otto Lewis and other earlier artists, who had painted the Indian chiefs and dignitaries involved in council meetings over which General Clark presided.

Catlin had with him some of his own paintings of the Indians on the nearby reservations — Senecas, Ottawas and others. General Clark viewed these with a knowing eye, then encouraged the young artist by telling him he was the first one to paint Indians as they really were. Other artists, General Clark said, made the Indians' faces all look alike.

This was just the kind of praise to fire George with enthusiasm for his work. Soon he was portraying old chiefs in gay ceremonial robes, young bucks in war paint and trappings, and an occasional squaw bearing her bright-eyed baby tied to the cradle-board on her back.

After a visit to his wife and family in the East, Catlin returned to St. Louis, still determined to go West and paint the primitive red men. He was invited to live in the mansion of Major Benjamin O'Fallon, General Clark's nephew. O'Fallon became an enthusiastic admirer of the artist's work and purchased a number of his Indian paintings.

In continuing to study the natives who came to Clark's office in St. Louis, Catlin found out a great deal about the Indians. One of the basic things he learned was that, with few exceptions, every Indian was ready for war – either by choice or by necessity. A warrior was one who had taken a scalp, while a brave was one who had gone to war but had taken no scalps nor killed an enemy. Catlin began to realize the great authority that the chiefs exercised, and the importance of the medicine-men in the affairs of the tribe.

Catlin's friendship with General Clark made it possible for him to attend, with the general, a treaty-making council meeting on the Upper Mississippi River in July, 1830. Here the head men of the Iowas, Missouris, Omahas, and of the Sauk and Fox tribe had gathered to arrange a sale of their lands to the United States Government. The tribesmen also wanted General Clark to settle many disputes over the whites invading their lands.

On this trip with the general, Catlin started painting Indians in their native surroundings. He had made many portraits of the red men at their treaty meetings with the whites, but now the young artist began seriously to plan an excursion into the wilderness two thousand miles away.

He made two shorter trips from St. Louis, one up the Missouri River to Leavenworth in northeastern Kansas. The cantonment at Leavenworth was a gathering-place for Indians of the many tribes in the area: Iowa, Delaware, Potawatomi, Shawnee, Kickapoo and others. Some of them were peaceful Indians who had been shifted by the government from eastern woodlands but Leavenworth was on the outer fringe of the western frontier, and often wild and warlike tribes from remote areas visited the fort.

Catlin painted a celebrated warrior, White Cloud of the Iowas, who sat for his portrait wearing his warpath regalia. It included a necklace of bear claws and many strings of wampum.

Another of his sitters was the Shawnee Prophet, who was a brother of Tecumseh, the famous Indian ally of the British in the capture of Detroit.

A Shawnee chief also sat for his portrait. He was an old man with white hair, fine face and ears split and weighted as was the custom of his tribe.

Catlin's next trip with General Clark was to the villages of the Kanza (sometimes called Konza or Kansas) tribe, on the Kansas River seventy miles west of the Missouri. He painted from life the head chief and many of his warriors.

On his return to St. Louis, Catlin reworked the pictures he had made. He did not receive pay for the Indian portraits unless they were sold outright to eastern collectors, so he was forced to paint portraits of white men to obtain living expenses. However, after he had painted General William Clark's portrait and that of General Winfield Scott, his work became very popular among prominent St. Louisians, and he was able to earn enough to line his pockets with money.

The artist was looking forward eagerly to further painting of the primitive western Indians as well as reporting on their

Comanche War Party Meeting the Dragoons *George Catlin*

ceremonials and other tribal customs. His great adventure into the far west began the next year, in the spring of 1831.

As his assemblage of Indian portraits grew, Catlin conceived the idea of a gallery of Indian pictures. It appealed to him as one way to acquaint the general public with the red men and their way of life. From this time on his great ambition was to build up an exhibit of Indian pictures, artifacts and relics which he could show in the East. He called it Catlin's Indian Gallery and it became his lifelong interest.

As soon as he finished the portraits of his white patrons in St. Louis, Catlin went back home to Pennsylvania to show his wife Clara his Indian paintings. He was elated with the beginning he had made on his Indian Gallery project.

When spring came, Catlin returned to St. Louis, again leaving his delicate young wife behind. It was considered impossible for a white woman to endure the hardships of western travel, so Clara did not accompany her husband on his venture into the wild country.

George had arranged to go with Major John Dougherty on an excursion up the Platte River to the villages of the Grand Pawnee, Oto, Omaha, and Missouri tribes, which were under the Major's supervision as Indian Agent. This trail led to the place where Fort Laramie was built in 1834. It later became a part of the Oregon Trail. Catlin and the Major rode up the Platte River, going from one village to the next, thus allowing the artist to paint portraits of the Oto, Omaha, and Grand Pawnee Indians of the region.

On this trip Catlin made a fine portrait of La-Doo-Ke-a (The Buffalo Bull), a Grand Pawnee of distinction. He wore his "medicine," the head of a buffalo, painted on his face and chest. Another sitter was Om-Pag-Ton-Ga (The Big Elk), a head chief of the Omahas. This leader made a fine speech declaring that no man of his tribe had ever harmed a white man, and he became known for his hospitality to white travelers.

Catlin also did a portrait of a celebrated Oto (or Otoe) warrior, No-Way-Ke-Sug-Gah (He Who Strikes Two At Once), wearing a necklace of bear's claws and holding his pipe in his hand. The colorful Oto garb, trimmed with many scalp locks and eagle feathers, made a vividly beautiful painting.

In addition to the portraits he painted in these first travels on the western frontier, Catlin gained a vast amount of information about the land and its inhabitants.

He tried to record the names of the various tribes and the individual tribesmen, a matter which had long confused white men. Many of the tribes were known by the names other tribes called them, although they called themselves something entirely different. Some tribes had been named by the early fur traders. For example, they called the Dakotah tribe "Sioux." After the United States Government moved to regulate the Indians, the groups, tribes, and bands were named in published reports. This added more confusion to identifying the groups.

As the white men crowded in on their lands and forced the Indians to move, some to merge with other small tribes, names and identities became even more of a problem. Catlin made efforts to correct some of the errors but his spelling was for the most part erratic and different from that carried on the government rolls.

One reason for the difficulty was that the Indians had no Christian names. A boy might be named for his father or his grandfather but his brothers and sisters did not have similar names. Whatever they were called, a qualifying word might be added, as The Fox, The Owl, One Who Runs Away, The Wise One. An individual might have several names: the one given at birth, that name as changed on going to war or on performing some notable feat, and the name as it stood on his becoming a chief. The Indians believed that names had power. They could be loaned or given away or discarded. However, it was not considered polite to address a man directly by his proper name. If used too often, the name might lose its power. Black Hawk, the famous chief of the Sauk and Fox tribe, had a number of names. He signed himself by several different names on different occasions.

3

UP THE MIGHTY MISSOURI

One of Catlin's friends in St. Louis was Pierre Chouteau, western manager of John Jacob Astor's far-flung empire, the American Fur Company. Chouteau, a member of the pioneer family of trappers and traders whose names dot the pages of the record of the early West, was in charge of all the company's trading posts along the Missouri and Platte Rivers and of the trapping operations in the whole Northwest.

In the summer of 1831, the fur company built a 130-foot boat — a double-deck, two-stack river steamboat called the *Yellow Stone*. They planned that the boat would carry a great load of supplies up the Missouri for two thousand miles to the mouth of the Yellowstone River where their farthest trading post, Fort Union, was located. From this post the trappers and traders would make their way into the unknown wilds of the westernmost prairies and the Rocky Mountains.

All the talk in St. Louis was about this daring adventure. The only other steamboat to attempt the trip had gone only as far as Council Bluffs, Iowa, from where the supplies and trade goods had to be transported across the country on pack horses or poled up the river in keel boats.

It seemed that everyone wanted to make this first trip, and
George Catlin was determined to do so. He had a promise from
Pierre Chouteau that they would try to make room for him
and his painting paraphernalia but George could not be certain he would be taken along until the boat was loaded and
ready to start.

The artist made a winter visit back east to see his beloved
Clara but he was so anxious to ride the *Yellow Stone* up the
Missouri that he returned to St. Louis quite a while before
spring. He had heard that the steamboat would be headed upriver as soon as the ice was gone in order to take advantage
of the high water. He didn't want to chance being late.

During the waiting period Catlin planned his campaign to
paint the tribes of the West. He would ride the *Yellow Stone*
as far as she went, quit the boat and paint the nearby Indians.
Then he would make trips out into the adjacent country,
painting and sketching.

When he had done this he would get a canoe and drift
downriver back to St. Louis. He planned to make it a leisurely
voyage so that he could paddle ashore to visit the various forts,
stopping at the Indian villages or at any other place which
merited his attention.

Catlin had it in mind to study the country as he moved up
the Missouri and to decide then where he would land on the
way down.

The *Yellow Stone* left St. Louis on March 26, 1832, with a
motley crowd of men aboard. With the exception of George
Catlin and Major John F. A. Sanford, the U. S. Indian agent
for the tribes of the Upper Missouri, they were French-
Canadian river men, hard-bitten white trappers of English or
Scotch descent, and half-breeds of various tribes who were to
do the work of building the fort.

The Major had with him a group of Indians whom he had

taken to Washington, D. C., the previous winter to meet the Great White Father and represent their tribes. He was returning them to their homes.

Included in the Indian band was a handsome young warrior, son of the chief of the Assiniboins, whose village was just below Fort Union. His name was Wi-jun-jon, translated as The Light. The name was also translated as The Pigeon's Egg Head and is so referred to in many books. Catlin persuaded him to don his native garb for a portrait. The costume was fresh and brilliant: leggings and shirt of mountain goatskin, trimmed with porcupine quills and locks from enemy scalps he had taken. He also wore eagle feathers and a robe made from the skin of a young buffalo on which was painted scenes from the battles he had fought in.

Living in Washington that winter as a guest of the Great White Father had changed The Light. He had discarded his classic native dress for a military full-dress uniform and was strutting about the deck of the steamer in fine blue broadcloth trimmed with gold braid, and a high crowned hat. A silver medal on a blue ribbon hung from his neck and a belt over his left shoulder supported a broadsword! By way of contrast with the portrait in Indian dress, Catlin painted him in this regalia with a blue umbrella in one hand and a fan in the other.

As the *Yellow Stone* huffed and puffed its way up the muddy Missouri, there was little action for Catlin until they stopped at the village of the Poncas, near the mouth of the Niobrara River in Nebraska. This was the dividing point between the white man's civilization and the native way of life.

The leader of the Poncas came aboard and Catlin talked with him through an interpreter. The Chief had a sad tale to relate to the always sympathetic Catlin. Said the chief, "My people are poor and hungry. Soon there will be no more Poncas. The buffalo which the Great Spirit provided for the

Indians once covered the green prairies but the white man has killed them all."

He pointed out that the young men of his tribe had been offered the white man's firewater and had become so fond of it that they had given away everything they owned for drink. Firewater had ruined many of his warriors and soon the rest would be destroyed, he said.

Before the *Yellow Stone* left the spot, the Poncas took down their skin lodges and moved on west where the game was more plentiful.

Wi-Jun-Jon (The Light) Going to and
Returning from Washington   *George Catlin*

Mandan Boys in Sham Fight *George Catlin*

Catlin learned something of the tragedy of Indian life when he found an old man of the Poncas who was being left behind. He had been a chief and a man of might, but now he was too old and feeble to keep up with the tribe. They were leaving him behind to starve. He had a fire and some sticks to burn, a few morsels of food and a dish of water, but no weapons with which to get game or to fend off wild animals. Catlin sat beside the dim-sighted old man, shook his hand, and let him know that he sympathized with him in his misfortune. Then Catlin went back to the steamboat to resume the journey, saddened but unable to do anything helpful.

When they were a thousand miles up the Missouri, the trip became an expedition into the untamed West. The overloaded *Yellow Stone* ran into sandbars, submerged trees and huge snags as it fought its way upriver.

The travelers began to see herds of wild game, buffalo, elk and deer, which showed their heels in panic at the sound of the puffing steamboat. The Indians in the villages they passed seemed even more frightened than the animals. As the steamer approached a large village, the artillery being taken to Fort Union (a twelve-pound cannon and three four-pound swivels) was fired rapidly to salute for the first time the shores of the mighty Missouri.

The *Yellow Stone* went aground before they reached Fort Pierre and they had to wait for a rise in the river to float her. Some of the men under Chouteau set out on foot to make a two-hundred-mile hike across the plains to the fort, located at the mouth of the Teton River, where a hunting party was encamped.

Catlin loaded his painting paraphernalia on the backs of several of the walkers, hung his sketchbook on his own back and started out with them, rifle in hand.

Tramping over the prairies tested the artist's legs and his endurance against that of the men who had spent most of their lives doing it.

After a week's march they located the Sioux camp of more than six hundred skin lodges at Fort Pierre. The Sioux, properly called Dakotah, were a large and warlike tribe who believed that taking a scalp entitled a warrior to the greatest degree of honor.

All the Plains Indians, Catlin learned, took scalps in battle or in any other way to denote the overcoming of an enemy! It is reported that this custom started with the eastern tribes who brought the heads of their enemies to show to their British allies as proof of their conquests. These were too messy and smelly for the English so the Indians compromised by merely taking scalps as evidence.

It is likely that this dreadful custom of scalping was the leading thing that triggered the hate and fear of the early white settlers for the redskins. Scalping victims were usually slain but sometimes they lived — objects of pity and revulsion.

There were rules and regulations as to what constituted a genuine "scalp." The palm-sized trophy was usually dried, then ornamented and displayed on the taker's person or horse. Occasionally, a scalp was buried after having been properly "danced."

Catlin noted that many of the Sioux warriors had guns, although the greater number of them hunted with bow and arrow and lance. They were such fine horsemen that they could kill game while racing their horses full speed. In person they were fine-looking, tall and straight and graceful in movement.

The first Sioux to sit for Catlin was The One Horn, a chief of the band, who wore a small shell hanging from a thong about his neck. It was his "medicine," handed down to him from his father, and he valued it highly. His long heavy hair, his reputation as a hunter, and the fact that he could run down a buffalo on his own two legs and then plunge a knife into its heart, had made him head man. Furthermore, his wigwam was decorated with scalps taken in battle and with other trophies.

Catlin went buffalo hunting with the Sioux and wrote a dramatic account of the hunt. He also painted stirring scenes of the tribesmen, bows in hand and arrows ready for instant use, guiding their horses to the right side of the racing buffalo and then, at the instant when the horse was passing, speeding an arrow into the buffalo's heart "to the feather." George Catlin, Buffalo Hunter, also made a sketch of himself concealed under a buffalo hide, stalking the huge beasts along with the Sioux.

When Catlin finished the painting of The One Horn, he invited several other chiefs to look at it. No Indian of this tribe had seen a portrait of anyone on canvas. They were so frightened and overcome that they clapped their hands over their mouths. When they left the artist's wigwam and told of what they had seen, it caused a terrific buzz of excitement.

Catlin had to display the portrait outside where all could examine it. The Indians were so impressed by the white man's ability that they gave him a title — Ea-cha-zoo-kah-wa-kon, The Medicine Painter. This elevation of a white to the rank of "medicine man" sent the tribal medicine men into a jealous rage. They told the warriors that bad luck and quick death would be the fate of anyone who permitted his body and soul to be pictured. "He can't even sleep at night," they said, pointing to the always-open eyes in the painting. At this the women and children who looked at the painting of their mighty chief, The One Horn, moaned and cried, and the bravest of the warriors avoided Catlin's glance.

Things looked black for the young artist. It seemed that his well-meant efforts had come to a dead end.

The white traders of the fort, who had been amused at the Indians' action, became alarmed for Catlin's safety. They combined their forces to talk with The One Horn and persuade the chief that he could suffer no harm from having sat for his portrait — that, instead, it was a great honor. The chief, finally convinced, made an oration to his people, saying that Catlin, a great medicine man of the whites, had come from a long distance to paint the portraits of the great men of the Sioux, that he would take the pictures back to his home for the white chiefs to see and admire.

The childlike Indians quickly changed their minds about the picture-making and some of the leaders hurried to their wigwams to dress in finest regalia for their own portraits.

Catlin's makeshift studio became a gathering-place for the notable men of all the many bands of Sioux. They crowded in to watch the medicine man at his work and waited to be sure they didn't miss their turn. The artist observed strict protocol as to rank and importance but when he suggested he would like to paint a woman of the tribe, the warriors hooted at the idea. They said it was an insult to them because the women had never taken a scalp; all they did was build fires, cook and dress the hides from the hunt. However, with his usual facility for making friends, Catlin overcame the objections of the warriors and was able to make some beautiful portraits of women of the tribe.

The warriors who sat for their pictures were so vain and so fond of their likenesses that they sometimes lay on the ground for days gazing at them and admiring them. They watched over the pictures to protect them from harm, believing that the portraits had life and if any injury were done to them the subject would suffer.

As time went on, George Catlin came to be so highly regarded for the "medicine" of his painting that the Indians honored him with a Dance of the Chieftains, the greatest compliment they could pay him.

The dance was held in front of the head chief's wigwam with people watching from the sidelines and the chiefs, in their best finery, doing the dancing. Catlin made a painting of the scene. The artist also painted the Bear Dance, which was usually given by the hunters several days before they set out on a bear hunt. Led by the chief medicine man dressed in a bear skin, and wearing bear masks over their faces, they danced and joined in songs to conciliate the Bear Spirit and bring success in hunting the ferocious animals. While the drums sounded, the dancers imitated the motions and sounds of the bear they were setting out to hunt.

Foot War Party in Council, Mandan   *George Catlin*

Another painting was of the Beggars Dance, an appeal to
the Great Spirit to touch the hearts of the rich and cause them
to give to the poor. It promised that the givers would be re-
warded by the Great Spirit for their generosity to the poor
and helpless.

The Scalp Dance, most important of all, was a wild celebra-
tion by a victorious war party. It was a tumult by torchlight
wherein young belles of the band were chosen to hold up the
gory scalps while the warriors gyrated around them, jumping
and stamping and yelling boasts of their brave deeds.

4

THE MEDICINE PAINTER
AT WORK

As MIGHT HAVE BEEN EXPECTED, Catlin's paintings led to jealousy and dissensions among the tribesmen. Many of them were torn between vanity and superstitious fear at having their portraits made. The medicine men told the sitters that after they died the portraits would live on as captives of the white men and cause the originals of the paintings much suffering.

When the artist was painting The Little Bear, a foremost chief of the Hunkpapa band of western Sioux, a tragic incident occurred which came close to ending Catlin's life. He had decided to paint a profile of the chief instead of full face and was working on it with the other Indians squatting inside the wigwam watching. Then the villain, in the form of The Dog, entered. He was a member of the Bad Arrow Points band, a surly fellow with few friends. The newcomer planted himself in front of The Little Bear and said, "The Little Bear is only half a man!" He pointed to the profile, which showed only one side of the chief's face. This remark brought on a battle of words between the two. The Dog had not been included among Catlin's subjects and he was determined to make the artist suffer.

After replying to the accusation by calling The Dog "an old woman and a coward," The Little Bear finished his sitting, approved the painting and presented Catlin with a fine buckskin shirt, decorated with porcupine quills and fringed with scalp locks from many enemy heads.

Then The Little Bear went to his own wigwam, loaded his flintlock gun and dropped a ball into the barrel. He followed the custom of the tribe by lying face down on the ground to petition The Great Spirit for help and protection. His wife, who knew nothing of the argument, saw his preparations and while he was praying, she shook the ball out of his rifle to keep the peace.

While The Little Bear was still praying, The Dog called from outside, "If The Little Bear be a whole man, let him come out and prove it." At that The Little Bear stepped outside his lodge. Both men fired at the same time but The Dog ran away unhurt and The Little Bear fell to the ground. The side of his face which was left out of the picture was shot away.

In the ensuing battle, the warriors of The Bad Arrow Points band were able to get away from the arrows and rifle balls of The Little Bear's band although one suffered a broken arm. The squaws had taken down the wigwams and all were able to make a hurried departure.

When The Little Bear died of his wound, his wife mourned and accused herself of being responsible for his death, however innocently. The warriors and friends of The Little Bear swore that The Dog should die for the slaying. All of the natives, their superstitions aroused by the death of the popular Little Bear, began to blame George Catlin and his picture "medicine" for the happening.

The traders and other white men, newly alarmed for Catlin's safety, urged him to collect his belongings and get ready to leave. Then they hurried the plans for the *Yellow Stone's* departure and the steamboat pulled out the following day.

Catlin, on his return to Fort Pierre several months later, learned the rest of the story. The followers of The Little Bear chased the Bad Arrow Points band and several battles ensued. In one of these The Little Bear's brother, The Steep Wind, was killed. His death and that of others were laid directly at the feet of the white "Medicine Painter" who had painted The Little Bear with only half a face. After holding a council, the Indians decreed death for George Catlin and also for The Dog. When he arrived at St. Louis, the artist was told that The Dog had been hunted down and killed. His death had ended the war between the two bands and they had become good friends again. Whether they had taken Catlin back into their good graces was not learned.

During his stay at Fort Pierre, Catlin was able to meet a party of Cheyennes who came from farther west to visit the trading post. Their land was blessed with an abundance of wild horses and they did a good business of trading these with the Sioux and the Mandans while warring with the neighboring Blackfeet to the north and the Pawnees to the south. The wife of the head chief of the Cheyennes was an attractive subject for Catlin's brush.

After leaving Fort Pierre, the *Yellow Stone* made only a few brief stops on the eight-hundred-mile journey up the Missouri River to Fort Union. It was near the end of the flood season and there was danger that the big steamboat might become stalled in low water and have to remain there until the next spring.

Catlin found that The Light was still on board, anxiously waiting for the boat to reach the Assiniboin village of his people. The handsome uniform which the President had given him in Washington was by now sadly wrinkled and stained from being worn day and night. His kid gloves were black with soil but he still sported the broadsword and sash. In his pockets were two bottles of firewater and he held a small keg of the potent liquor under his arm.

When the *Yellow Stone* tied up at the Assiniboin village, more than a thousand of the eight thousand members of the tribe were there to meet their chief's son, including his wife and children and other relatives and friends.

Catlin watched The Light walk ashore in his ridiculous getup and stand alone on the bank. Neither his wife, Chincah-pee, The Fire Bug, nor any others of the crowd spoke to him. Anxious as they were to hear about his long trip and the visit to the Great White Father in Washington, the shock of seeing him in his bedraggled white man's uniform with umbrella and fan was too much for their understanding. After half an hour of gazing at him in silence, the Indians yielded to their curiosity and began asking questions of the returning warrior.

The *Yellow Stone* pulled out quickly but later on Catlin learned the rest of The Light's story. It seemed that the tribesmen were unable to swallow the wild tales that the erstwhile hero told about the white men and their strange ways. The whole tribe declared him a liar, who had been among the whites (who were great liars) and had learned nothing except to come home and tell lies. The Light became very unpopular but he still strutted about with his tokens of civilization and told stories of the manners and habits of the men in Washington.

When the keg and bottles of firewater were empty, he found that all his friends had deserted him. His wife had cut off his frock coat at the waist to make herself a fine pair of leggings and used the gold lace from his hat for new garters. He still had the umbrella, which he carried over his head at all times. On the buffalo hunts he did nothing but talk of the places he had seen and the things he had done. At last the prestige he had once enjoyed turned to actual dislike, and the tribe eventually destroyed him for being the most impossible liar and utterly worthless person they had ever had among their number.

The *Yellow Stone* arrived at Fort Union, two thousand miles from St. Louis, on June 26, 1832. Catlin and the others in the group were greeted with yells of welcome from the fur company men and cannon were fired in honor of the occasion. The native Indians lined the shore to see the big boat unload its passengers and freight. Most of them were torn between fright and amazement.

Catlin described Fort Union, built in 1829, as a "very beautiful fort." In 1832 it was the chief trading place for the area and a rendezvous for several large tribes who traveled far to visit it. They might be deadly enemies elsewhere but the vicinity of the trading post was held inviolate as peaceful ground. Blackfeet, Crows, Assiniboins and Crees all camped nearby.

The fort, a stone building two hundred feet square and enclosed in a stockade for protection, contained ten log houses, a force of fifty men and a hundred or more horses. The agent in charge of the fort, though a sharp bargainer when dealing with the Indians and dedicated to taking over the Northwest from them, was impressed with Catlin and his paintings. He offered the artist every assistance in his endeavor to paint the magnificent scenery about him and the picturesque red men in their daily lives.

At Fort Union the American Fur Company dealt mostly with the Blackfeet and Crows, who claimed the land west to the Rocky Mountains, all fine beaver country.

The Blackfeet and the related Piegans and the Bloods from farther north were a large and warlike tribe with a high degree of culture according to Indian standards. They were already beginning to feel the pressure of the white men's dominance and openly resented it. They wanted to come to Fort Union to trade but warned the traders they would not tolerate the fur company's men trapping in their territory. They stated they would kill any white men they caught taking beaver or other game.

Already some fifteen to twenty company men had lost their lives in disregarding the warning. However, Catlin felt that the Indians' desire for trinkets and trade goods and their love of firewater would weaken their will to resist, and in the end the whites would devour the wealth of prairie and stream and leave the red men to starve in a desolate wasteland.

The makeshift studio set up for Catlin at the fort was a place of great mystery to the natives who crowded around him to watch. Enemies jostled and glared at each other but since all weapons had to be left in the arsenal while in the fort, the Indians could only trade looks of hatred and threatened revenge.

The chiefs decided which of the warriors were worthy of having their portraits done by Catlin. While the artist painted, the Indians took turns telling of the battles they had fought. They calmly smoked their pipes and displayed the scalplocks sewed to the seams of their shirts and leggings as proof of their bravery and the victories they had won. As they were unarmed, existence in the fort was peaceful but all were mindful that there would be another day when they would meet on the plains and arrows would fly again.

One of Catlin's most appealing portraits was that of a chubby six-year-old boy who posed with his bow and quiver of arrows and his robe of raccoon skins. He was the grandson of the head chief of the Blackfeet, but too young to have a tribal name. The boy's father was dead and when the old chief died, the little boy would inherit the position of chief.

He had been stolen by the Crows on three different occasions and retaken by the Blackfeet after fierce battles.

At this time he had just been left at the fort under the protection of the whites to remain until he was old enough to become chief.

Another subject for the artist was the chief medicine man of the Blackfeet, The White Buffalo. Catlin painted him wearing all the colorful regalia of his mysterious rites and also made a sketch of his actual performance over the body of a dead tribesman.

"Medicine" played an important part in the lives of the Indians. It stood for mystery and the supernatural rather than drugs, but the medicine men often acted as doctors and healers. Each tribe had its own sacred medicine — unusual objects such as the hide of an albino (white) buffalo or deer, a snake with many rattles, or an enormous skull. These were kept in elaborately decorated bundles as objects of veneration.

In addition, each man had his own personal medicine bag to which he prayed for protection throughout his life. This last medicine was usually obtained as a result of his manhood test. The young Indian "made his medicine" by wandering alone in the desert or wilderness without food or water for several days. During this time he prayed to The Great Spirit and lay on the ground waiting for a vision which would indicate what his medicine should be. If he dreamed of an animal, bird or snake, it became the object of his medicine. If he had an hallucination induced by lack of food and water, or if he pretended to have one, he still must make his medicine before he could go home. He always came up with something as a basis for his medicine bag. This fetish was to be his guardian spirit for his entire life and it was buried with him to guide him into the red men's heaven.

Indian Boy   *George Catlin*

As the honored "medicine painter," Catlin was allowed to see and sketch the rites in which the young men of the Sioux tribe underwent ordeals of torture in order to become braves. The Sun Dance was a bloody performance in which the youths' friends and relatives and the medicine men danced, yelled and shook rattles while the initiates hung suspended from poles and looked at the sun from dawn to dusk. Thongs were run through slits in the flesh of their chests, arms or backs. At the end of the day, the young men were cut down from the poles and each of them was given presents and the name of a medicine man. They were honored for the rest of their lives. If an unfortunate youth failed to last through the day, fainted or cried out, he was disgraced in the eyes of the whole tribe.

Other tribes held similar ceremonies at the time when their Indian boys were supposed to become men.

Catlin's notes describing his trip up and down the Missouri River were published as letters to the Editor of the *New York Commercial Advertiser* between July 24, 1832 and February 20, 1833. Later they were published as a part of his two-volume book, *Letters and Notes on the Manners, Customs and Conditions of the North American Indians.* This was gotten out by Catlin in London, 1841, and is regarded as the best record ever made of the Mandan, Crow, Blackfoot, Knisteneux (Cree), Sioux, Assiniboin, Minnetaree, Arikara, Ponca and Iowa tribes.

Like all artists Catlin had an inquiring mind about the things that interested him, and his friendship with the red men enabled him to observe their religious habits, customs, taboos and other details of their daily lives. He made notes on such matters as their facial characteristics (eyes, nose, teeth, hair), their lack of beards, their small families, their childbirth rituals, their bathing, their tribal records and their games and ceremonies.

The hasty sketches he made when pressed for time were filled in later from memory and from the notes in his sketchbooks. He also carried pieces of unmounted canvas so that the pictures, as they were painted and dried, could be rolled up and packed in a round tin case he carried on his back.

When fall was in the air, Catlin and his two trapper companions, Baptiste and Bogard, gathered their belongings, including the priceless collection of paintings and the Indian relics, and set out downriver for St. Louis. They had plenty of food with them, described as "dried buffalo tongues, a dozen or two of beaver tails and a good supply of pemmican, (which was a mixture of dried pounded meat and berries)." Besides this, they also carried in the canoe three tin cups, a coffee pot, one tin plate, a frying pan and a tin kettle. Catlin visited at Indian camps along the way and stopped to hunt various animals, like buffalo, elk, antelope, grizzly bear and mountain sheep.

After a week of travel the party reached the huge Mandan village on the river bank across from the present site of Bismarck, North Dakota.

The Mandans, a good-looking and highly intelligent people, fascinated Catlin. He spent two weeks with them, painting and making notes of the festivals, ceremonies and other tribal gatherings. He also went hunting and as a highlight of his stay visited with an ancient chief of the Minnetarees who had seen Lewis and Clark when they stopped at the Mandan village during the winter of 1804-1805. His name was The Black Moccasin.

Catlin and the trappers parted from the Mandans with friendly farewells, and their canoe was almost out of sight downriver when the three men heard yells and saw the Indians racing after them and waving robes for them to stop. Catlin steered his boat to the bank to talk with them. They said they wanted to take back the picture of the young girl which Catlin had painted. The girl was sick and they feared that she would die because the artist's medicine was too great — the picture was too much like her.

When the interpreter with the party explained what the Indians wanted, Catlin unrolled his bundle of portraits and placed the picture in their hands, although he was reluctant to part with it. The Indians dashed off and Catlin thankfully got under way again. He learned later that the girl died and that he, the artist, was held responsible for her death.

5

CATLIN WITH THE DRAGOONS

CATLIN SPENT THE WINTER of 1833 in Florida with his wife, Clara. The warm sun helped to restore him to better health and in the spring his thoughts were all for setting out on a search for new Indian portraits to add to his gallery.

In February of 1834 he obtained official permission to accompany the First Regiment of Mounted Dragoons (so called from the dragon insignia stamped on early guns) on an expedition into the Southwest.

Clara Catlin went to St. Louis, then to Alton, Illinois, to stay with friends until her husband should return from the expedition.

George, with a helper and companion, Joe Chadwick, joined the regiment at Fort Gibson in the territory of Arkansas. This fort, established ten years before, was the farthest southwest outpost of the United States territory in 1834.

Many of the numerous Indians around the fort had been moved there from their eastern locations. Catlin spent two months traveling among the tribes, painting and making notes. He visited Cherokees, Choctaws, Creeks, Chickasaws, Senecas,

Delawares and others. He painted Cherokee chief Col-lee and
a Creek chief called The Great King. He also did portraits of
handsome young chief Clermont and of Tal-lee, a famous
warrior, both of the Osage tribe.

Catlin was so intrigued by the ball-play of the Choctaws
that he often rode for miles to attend a game. The ball, in this
game, was caught in a net at the end of a stick and thrown
from there untouched by hands, something like modern
lacrosse. The game was customarily preceded by a ball-play-
ing dance in which everyone — spectators, players and referees
— took part. Then it became a wild scramble and usually
ended in a fight.

While Catlin was at Fort Gibson, he bought a horse,
"Charlie," for the sum of one hundred and fifty dollars. The
artist described Charlie, a cream-colored mustang with long
black tail and mane, as a complete horse. Charlie had everything and Catlin rode him and made friends with him for
several weeks before the regiment pulled out.

Finally the regiment of dragoons was lined up ready for
inspection by General Henry Leavenworth before venturing
into the wilds of the Comanche and Pawnee territory.

Catlin, ever alert to the appeal of fine horses, noted that
each company's mounts were of a different color. In one
company all horses were white, in another all were black.
There were companies with greys, others with sorrels or
cream-colored mounts. The dragoons presented a dashing
appearance as the expedition moved out with banners flying.

The artist and his friend Joe were with the headquarters
company and for the first few days they enjoyed the glimpses
of buffalo and other game which high-tailed over the plains
at sight of them. Their packhorse carried their bearskin
bedding, coffee pot and frying pan, and they took side trips
to inspect places of interest while the mile-long train of dra-

goons wound its way over the green prairie. Before long a mysterious fever struck men and horses and brought down some of the stoutest. Catlin was one of the unfortunates. He shared a tent with the commanding officer, General Henry Leavenworth, who was very ill. The general ordered that all the men able to sit their horses make the advance into the Comanche territory as planned. There he hoped the climate would be healthier.

Catlin summoned all his strength and encouraged by his friend Joe, rode with the able-bodied men of the expedition under the leadership of Colonel Grenville Dodge, into what proved to be an equally hot, dry country. There was little water available and most of that was unfit for human consumption. They lost more men and horses and finally the artist again became so ill he had to be carried in a litter.

However, at the time the dragoons sighted a war party of Comanches, Catlin was able to take part in what he called an inspiring and beautiful scene. Colonel Dodge halted his men and, accompanied by Catlin, rode forward with an escort carrying a white flag. When they were a short distance from the Indians, the leader of the war party, riding a fine white horse and carrying a banner on his lance, galloped up to the whites and extended his hand to Colonel Dodge. The men of the escort then grasped the hand of the Indian leader, and as the regiment pulled up to the colonel, each warrior rode along the ranks and shook hands with every man.

One of Catlin's finest paintings records this scene.

After a parley and peace-pipe smoke, the dragoons rode along with the war party to their distant village. The buffalo were abundant and the Comanches showed off their skill in hunting and in capturing wild horses.

They were expert riders, as they demonstrated for the artist. An Indian would hang with a heel over the horse's back, body along the animal's side, carrying bow and arrows and long lance, and at the moment of passing his prey would deal a death blow. He could reverse to the other side of the horse and do the same thing.

Catlin's curiosity led him to investigate this feat. He bribed a young Comanche with tobacco and got close enough to see the short halter of horsehair which went around the neck of the horse. He observed that both ends of the halter were braided into the mane, leaving a loop under the horse's neck. The rider's elbow slipped into this sling to take the weight of his body on the upper arm. His heel over the horse's back steadied the man and helped him to straighten up on the animal.

Despite the fact that he was still a very sick man, Catlin moved around among the Comanches and made sketches and notes. He painted a huge chief known as The Mountain of Rocks, a three-hundred-pound Indian with a chin beard, a feature so rare that he is the only Indian so adorned in all Catlin's paintings of Plains Indians.

The dragoons were still sickening and dying from the mysterious malady. Colonel Dodge grew anxious to complete his mission by visiting the Pawnee Picts at the edge of the Rockies. What to do about the litter cases and the artist?

Finally, he decided to leave behind in a brush shelter at the Comanche Camp all the men who were not able to sit in the saddle. Catlin, try as he would, could not mount Charlie even after his friend Joe had saddled the horse for him. Instead the artist sent Joe Chadwick with a sketchbook and note-pad to record what he could of the Pawnee village and its inhabitants.

The trip was so rugged for the dragoons that they barely made it to the Pawnee village in starving condition. By orders of the head chief, the squaws brought loads of dried buffalo meat and ears of fresh corn to revive them.

After Colonel Dodge had met in council with the chiefs of the Pawnees, he hurried to get his one hundred able-bodied men and his sick dragoons started for home, escorted by two chiefs of the Pawnees as far as the Comanche camp. At a stop on the Canadian River, they received word of the death of General Leavenworth and others of the men who had been left at the first sick camp.

Catlin suffered a relapse and his condition became so serious that he was put in a baggage wagon and made the journey back to Fort Gibson in a semiconscious state, jolted and bounced until the skin of his wasted limbs was worn off. Many soldiers died on this trip and were buried with military honors.

In the healthier climate of the fort, Catlin, in spite of his frail constitution, began to improve in health and soon was able to mount Charlie and set out for St. Louis by a direct route across the country.

He had with him a small compass, ammunition, food and the same indomitable spirit that had sustained him in illness and brought him through innumerable perils. Catlin related that he reached the Osage River when it was over its banks from recent rains. He collected wood and made a raft to bear his clothes and saddle and other possessions. Then he stripped and drove Charlie across, swimming behind him and pushing the raft across the river to the other shore.

Catlin eventually reached Boonville, a settlement on the Missouri, and went on to Alton (across the Mississippi River from St. Louis). There he was reunited with his wife, the lovely and patient Clara. Then the Catlins went to Florida for the winter to allow the artist to build up his health again.

When spring came, George was off on more travels, this time with his wife. They went back to St. Louis, then to Fort Snelling, near St. Paul, Minnesota, where the United States Government kept troops to enforce peace among the tribes in the area. The region was rich in subjects for the artist's brush. He and his wife enjoyed a period of relaxation visiting the Indian camps and observing the games and contests and dances of the natives.

It was here that Catlin, with his usual proficiency in doing what other men did, obtained a birch-bark canoe from the Chippewas and learned to handle it as well as any of the Indians. He made a number of trips by canoe while his wife remained with friends.

Kee-o-kuk, first chief of the Sauk and Fox tribe, sat for his portrait in all the fine trappings of his wardrobe. So did others of his band before the artist went back to join his wife.

After this, Catlin made his historic trip to the sacred Red Pipestone quarry, which is in the southwest corner of Minnesota. On August 17, 1836, he and a companion set out to visit the quarry in spite of warnings from various tribesmen that they would not be allowed to see the place.

For centuries the pipestone quarries had supplied the Indians of many tribes with material for their ceremonial pipes. Smoking the pipe was an integral part of their civic and religious life. It sealed the signing of treaties between the Indians and the whites or between hostile tribes. It was the means by which every warrior petitioned The Great Spirit for good luck in hunting and in battle, and for protection from storms and other disasters. The red pipestone, sometimes pink or terra-cotta in color, when first mined from the rock strata was soft enough to be carved into the desired shape.

Catlin was always popular with the Indians he visited, but no one of them was willing to risk incurring the wrath of the spirits by directing the artist to the secret quarry. In fact, they threatened him and his companion with dire results if they did not turn back.

George Catlin had faced danger many times in his excursions among the Indians so the threats did not scare him. He was not to be turned aside from something he wanted, but it is unlikely he would have located the quarry without help. Luckily he ran across a part-Indian employe of the fur company who led him to the spot. The artist was deeply impressed with the brooding spirit of the quarry and the many hieroglyphics on the surface of the rocks: totems and other marks left by tribesmen over the centuries. He collected some specimens to take with him. Afterwards he analyzed them to satisfy his own considerable curiosity. Many years later the pipestone was named catlinite in memory of him, and this is its scientific name today.*

From the secluded area of the quarry, Catlin and his companion paddled downriver to Rock Island, Illinois, and witnessed the ceremonies, dances and parades which marked the creation of the Territory of Wisconsin. It had been carved from the lands of the Sauk and Fox nation.

When the artist arrived in St. Louis on a river steamer he found that a large number of his paintings and some Indian material had been stolen from his stateroom. The loss of his paintings and other items so alarmed Catlin that he packed up all the things he had stored in St. Louis and took them to Albany.

On September 25, 1837, he opened an exhibition in New York City, with himself as lecturer. The admission price was fifty cents. Catlin's Indian Gallery thus became the first "Wild West" spectacle ever shown in the United States. At first it aroused great interest and made a good profit but less than a year later in April, 1838, he was forced to move it for financial

---

* Note — The old St. Joseph Museum at St. Joseph, Missouri, has on exhibit a fine specimen of a catlinite pipe. It has a stem two feet long and a bowl shaped like an egg with the top sliced off. The color is a beautiful soft rose and the pipe resembles a piece of highly polished wood. There seems to be little interest in the sacred quarry today and no organized effort to preserve it.

reasons. He went to Washington, D. C., hoping to sell the gallery intact to the United States Government, but he could get no encouragement there. He then moved the gallery to Baltimore, to Philadelphia, and later to Boston.

When interest in his exhibition flagged and his expenses became too heavy, Catlin decided on a bold move. In November 1839, he leased a hall in Piccadilly and took his collection to London. He showed it there to enthusiastic crowds for three profitable years.

Catlin's book, *Letters and Notes on the Manners, Customs and Conditions of the North American Indian,* was published at his own expense in London, October, 1841. It had a fine reception.

With his gallery and his book bringing him fame and fortune, Catlin was able to have his wife and children, three daughters and one son, his namesake George, join him in England. There they enjoyed a brief period of prosperity. Later, as people tired of the exhibition, Catlin moved his family and the gallery to Paris.

In France, Catlin's Indian Gallery was received with great acclaim for a time. Then as new sensations caught the public fancy, the show began to lose money. Expenses were heavy and Catlin met with dire misfortune. His wife, Clara, died of pneumonia on July 28, 1845, and his little son died soon after. The artist was torn between concern for the three pretty daughters and worry over the failure of his efforts to sell his collection.

During the winter of 1847-1848 there was political upheaval in Paris and Catlin was forced to flee to London with his three little girls and his gallery. He was in desperate financial straits but he managed to rent a studio with living quarters. There he set up his Indian pictures and relics and made a scanty living by charging small admission fees.

Handicapped by his growing deafness and the indifference of the public, Catlin continued to work on copies of his Indian paintings. He made a few small sales but finally had to place the gallery in pawn to get money for living expenses. He had counted heavily on selling the entire collection to the United States Government, and there was a bill before the Congress of 1851-1852 to purchase it but the bill was defeated by one vote. With that, all Catlin's creditors pounced upon his gallery. It was taken over for debt and stored. In 1852 a wealthy American, Joseph Harrison, paid the indebtedness and had the gallery shipped to Philadelphia where it was housed in his foundry.

Clara Catlin's brother, Dudley Gregory, was a wealthy and influential man. The entire Gregory family had become critical of Catlin and his financial difficulties and when they learned of the failure of the bill to purchase the gallery, Dudley Gregory hurried to England to get possession of the Catlin daughters. They were spirited out of London and put on a ship bound for New York before their father realized it. He never saw them again until he went back to New York in the last year of his life.

Penniless and deaf as he was, Catlin seemed at the end of his career but he still carried in his heart the flame of his sympathetic understanding and concern for the Indians. He continued to write about them and to make copies of his Indian sketches, selling these for small sums on which he lived.

In 1853 Catlin became interested in hunting gold in Venezuela and made a trip there. He found no gold, but he did find primitive Indians and other subjects for his brush. With a husky companion to carry the painting paraphernalia, he wandered over thousands of miles of wilderness. He visited the west coast of the United States after that, and then went on farther north.

He returned to Europe in 1858, settling in Brussels where he made a scanty living by selling drawings of his paintings. During this period he wrote three books about Indians. He talked continually about his gallery and showed great concern about the ultimate fate of his paintings — his "life's work."

Catlin was nearly seventy-seven years old and quite deaf when he journeyed to New York to see his daughters. He died in Jersey City, New Jersey, on December 23, 1872. His last words were, "What will become of my gallery?"

Catlin's original Indian Gallery was presented to the Smithsonian Institution by the heirs of Joseph Harrison on May 19, 1879.

Today the restored paintings are a part of the heritage of the American people. They have served as an inspiration and guide to every important painter of western scenes. His writings have been used by generations of historians, ethnologists and novelists. He is known as the dean of Indian painters, not only because he was the first to see the artistic side of the color-loving and picturesque western Indians, but also because he was their devoted and enthusiastic friend.

6

Karl Bodmer, 1809-1893
FIRST FOREIGN ARTIST
IN THE WEST

UNKNOWN TO GEORGE CATLIN, another artist of great talent was following close on his heels.

Karl Bodmer was a twenty-three-year old student in Paris when he met Prince Alexander Philip Maximilian of Weid-Neuweid and accepted a commission to act as artist-recorder for him on a trip to the United States. Bodmer, a well mannered young dandy, was to become the first foreign artist to paint our American Indians.

He had never been in America and was pleased with the idea of being associated with a titled, well-known man of scientific achievements in an adventure so unusual and so distant. No doubt he also considered the money offered sufficient inducement to leave the refinements and pleasures of Barbizon, site of an art colony just outside Paris, where he was already an established member.

At this time it was customary for men of wealth and position to sponsor promising young artists — that is, to purchase their pictures or commission them to do other work. For many struggling young painters, poets, writers or singers, a rich pa-

53

tron was necessary in order to live until they became well-known and prosperous.

Prince Maximilian had gained a reputation among ethnologists for an 1815-1816 trip he had taken into the wilds of Brazil to study the primitive tribes in that land. The unknown territory of North America offered him an additional challenge. He sought out young Bodmer, the best artist he could locate, to paint a picture record of the natives, the animals and other physical aspects of the nearly unexplored West. These would go into a folio "Atlas" and illustrate the book he meant to write about his North American journey.

The two men landed in Boston on July 4, 1832 and began to plan their trip. They found they would not be able to start the journey until the spring of 1833 when the floods would allow the Steamer *Yellow Stone* to get over the shallows in the river. This was the same steamer which had taken Catlin on his first trip to the West.

Camp of the Gros Ventres of the Prairie   *Karl Bodmer*

Fort Clark, 1834   *Karl Bodmer*

In the months of waiting for spring, Prince Maximilian visited the cities of the East, meeting with other ethnologists and studying exhibits in Boston, Philadelphia and New York. Bodmer took advantage of the waiting period to go down to New Orleans on a river steamer and visit the French-speaking citizens of that lively city. Since he had lived in Paris, it is likely the young Swiss artist spoke both French and German, as did his patron. At that time, every educated man was expected to speak at least two languages besides his native tongue.

As a result of his trip to New Orleans, Bodmer already had some grasp of the size and variety of the United States when he rejoined Prince Maximilian in the spring.

They started their journey on April 10, 1833, and found they had plenty of company on the *Yellow Stone*. About one hundred men, French-Canadian employes of the American Fur Company called "engagés" were aboard. A large crowd of St. Louisians gathered along the banks to witness the departure, wish them luck and fire a parting salute.

The *Yellow Stone* moved up the Big Muddy (Missouri) River, along which Bodmer was to find Indians in abundance at every stop.

Delighted, the young artist got out his sketching materials and exulted in the richness of the magnificent scenery and the novelty of the copper-skinned natives. With their colorful garb of hides, feathers and fur, the Indians presented an opportunity for him which his friends in Barbizon might well have envied.

It is likely that the elegant clothing in which Bodmer started his journey to America had by now given way to something more practical for the frontier. Most of the white men in the West wore fringed buckskin shirts and pants and moccasins, as Catlin did in a portrait painted by his friend William H. Fisk, in 1849.

Prince Maximilian appears not to have taken his princely garb. He had no velvet cloak, plumed hat, or lace-trimmed satin breeches with him. He is described as being around fifty and wearing a slouch hat, an old rusty coat, and trousers liberally spotted with grease. His interest was in hunting specimens for his collections and in keeping the artist, Bodmer, working at top speed.

By the time the steamer reached Fort Pierre, it was loaded with buffalo hides and furs obtained by its owners from Indians and trappers along the way. To Prince Maximilian and the artist Bodmer, each transaction represented not a financial opportunity but a scientific and artistic one.

The *Yellow Stone* headed back to St. Louis with its load of furs. The less conspicuous but ultimately more valuable burden of canvasses, sketches and scientific notes, made by the two Europeans in the three weeks while the boat struggled up the Missouri, went along with them on the next stage of their journey.

Fort Mackenzie, August 28th, 1833   *Karl Bodmer*

To travel in the West in 1833, it was necessary to have the help and protection and, more important, the sanction of the fur companies. With the possible exception of Fort McKenzie, the forts, which were also trading posts, had been set up by the American Fur Company and were maintained with forces of many employes as storage places for furs and homes for the traders, trappers and hunters.

The forts also furnished shelter and accommodations with some of the comforts of civilization for travelers in the region. Since there was no other place to meet, eat, smoke and tell tall tales of adventure, the forts dispensed hospitality to visitors without regard to a man's station in life.

Fort Pierre was in Sioux territory with Indians all around it. A village of Teton and Yankton Sioux was nearby, and Bodmer painted some of his finest portraits during this stay. Since they were to be used in illustrating Prince Maximilian's book on ethnology, they were presented with exactness and care, in a formal fashion some called "stiff" or "wooden." In later works, however, Bodmer demonstrated that he possessed an imaginative talent capable of portraying dynamic and even savage action.

After three weeks the steamer *Assiniboin* arrived, and Bodmer and his patron continued their journey upriver to Fort Clark, where the steamer made a brief stay. It was a two-weeks trip for the boat, which was delayed by sandbars, low water and snags (downed trees) in the river. At the many stops along the way, Bodmer made sketches of the vegetation, while Prince Maximilian clambered up and down hills and gulleys or high-tailed it over the prairie in search of specimens for his studies.

In addition to the artist Bodmer, Prince Maximilian had with him a servant, Dreidroppel, and is said to have kept the air thick with shouts and orders urging on the two to more work, more specimens and more paintings.

There was a big Mandan camp at Fort Clark. Catlin had been there the year before and Bodmer made sketches of many of the natives who had also posed for Catlin. Bodmer liked the friendly Mandans and painted some of his outstanding pictures while in their midst. Among these were "Buffalo Dance of the Mandans," and "Interior of the Hut of a Mandan Chief."

Before Bodmer had seen all he wanted to see and paint at Fort Clark, the *Assiniboin* was ready to move on. Furs were the business of the American Fur Company. No mere artist or ethnologist, no matter how distinguished in the world of art and science, could stay the wheels of commerce, especially when commerce owned the boat.

On board were two Blackfeet. One of them sat for Bodmer but the other refused because it was strange "medicine" and might get him killed. After six days of travel they reached

Interior of the Hut of a Mandan Chief   *Karl Bodmer*

Fort Union, arriving there June 24th. This was the largest of
the river forts and had a force of a hundred employes, plus
Indians, half-breeds, white traders and the partisans (the men
who ran the place). The fort had a stock of many thousands
of dollars worth of trade goods. It attracted not only the surrounding Assiniboins but other tribes from outside the area,
even as far north as Canada.

There was constant activity at Fort Union — traders coming
and going and Indians moving in and out. It would seem that
Prince Maximilian could have found here enough material to
last him for years but the lively and dedicated prince wanted
to go on and see all there was to be seen in the upper reaches
of the Missouri River.

So it was arranged. On July 6th, the factor at Fort McKenzie
and an assistant, with Bodmer and his patron and Dreidroppel

Bison Dance of the Mandans   *Karl Bodmer*

and a boat's crew of fifty-seven men, set out to make their way to Fort McKenzie by keelboat. For more than a month the crew pulled and hauled and poled the keelboat upriver, a slow and laborious process.

Bodmer, in response to his patron's urging, painted and sketched at top speed, putting the tortured badlands on canvas while Prince Maximilian gathered specimens of buffalo, bear, bighorn sheep, even snakes, for his study of the country's resources. He loaded the boat with his booty.

When they reached Fort McKenzie they found only twenty-seven men representing the American Fur Company. The entire population of the fort, with the men's Indian wives and children and relatives, was only fifty-three. This was a small group indeed to carry on trade with the surrounding Blackfoot tribe and their neighbors, the Flatheads, the Nez Perces, Kootenais and to the south and west, the Utes, Snakes and Crows, all warlike and potentially dangerous customers.

While Bodmer painted and sketched the exciting life around Fort McKenzie, Prince Maximilian was everywhere taking note of the ways and means of Indian life. He watched the factor haggle with the temperamental chiefs of various tribes and got a lesson in trading ammunition, scalping knives and foofaraw (cheap finery such as beads and red calico) for buffalo robes and beaver and other furs.

Moennitarri Warrior in Dog Dance   *Karl Bodmer*

The Europeans also got in on a tribal battle between the Blackfeet and several hundred Assiniboins and Crees. On August 29, while the Blackfeet were sleeping, their camp was attacked, their tents destroyed, and many of them were wounded in a sneak attack. As soon as it was discovered, the Fort McKenzie men rushed to their posts on the roof and saw that the fort was surrounded by hostile Indians. The factor ordered the gates of the fort opened so that the wounded Blackfeet could find refuge inside, and then every man rushed to the roof or the walls to ward off the hordes of attackers.

Bodmer and the prince watched the fierce fighting from a safe vantage point. It is likely that the artist was making sketches of the scene while the Indians were killing and being killed, for he painted an outstanding picture of this battle for the *Atlas* which was published as an accompaniment to Prince Maximilian's book of his travels.

As the battle raged, Blackfeet scouts on horseback raced through the enemy to try to get help from their tribe's big camp, ten miles away.

Finally, the warriors from the main camp, with warpaint hardly dry on their faces, rode up yelling and firing their guns and shooting arrows. With their help, the attackers were routed and the Blackfeet proceeded to gather many Cree and Assiniboin scalps.

The short but bloody war ended with about forty Blackfeet killed, including women and children. There was yelling, howling and the mourning of the women along with the frenzied chanting and gyrating of the medicine men. All these things were closely observed by ethnologist Prince Maximilian and his artist. One of the chiefs who had been in the midst of the battle assured Bodmer that his portrait, painted the day before, was the medicine that had saved his life.

It is not known whether this grisly experience caused a

Indians Hunting the Bison   *Karl Bodmer*

change of plans or whether Fort McKenzie had gotten enough
of the visitors but in the first week of September Prince Maximilian and his companions loaded a mackinaw boat with his
collection of specimens, said good-bye to the Blackfeet and
started downriver. They had with them an experienced voy-
ageur (river man) and a three-man crew and arrived safely at
Fort Union for a month's stay.

During the thirty-days visit at Fort Union, the Prince re-
checked his collection, added to it and made notes. Bodmer
worked on his water colors and sketches and probably dreamed
of the day when he would be back at Barbizon.

Bodmer's critics have said he was a cold man and a drafts-
man rather than an artist. It is probably true that he did not
have the intense interest in the Indian that kept Catlin painting
Indians for the rest of his life, but when a scene touched Bod-

mer's imagination, his talent and his training brought into
being an unsurpassed picture of the West. Then too most of
his water colors were meant to be illustrations. He was being
paid to illustrate Prince Maximilian's book and to record
scientific facts, and he did that beautifully, and in true likeness.

In comparing the two early artists, some critics say that
Bodmer's buffalo are not as good as Catlin's — which is under-
standable since the Swiss artist probably never saw a buffalo
until he had left St. Louis for the West — and that his horses
are not as horsey as Catlin's. Nevertheless, his few landscapes
and scenes of savage action gave the public a conception of a
strange and wild country which caught their imagination. By
many authorities he is considered the only artist who truly
interpreted the "Old West."

No one can quarrel with the perfection of his detailed
drawings which delighted Prince Maximilian and all who saw
them. The items of costume: quill trim, thongs of rawhide
with dangling hair, headdress with horns, feathers or fur, warbonnet, ceremonial lance with streamers of scalps, medicine
bag, and painting on face and body were finely executed.

On October 20, 1833, the Prince Maximilian party left Fort
Union and went downriver to Fort Clark, near where the
Mandan village was located. On this second visit to Fort Clark,
Bodmer found many subjects for fine paintings. The Mandans,
whom Catlin had immortalized, also fascinated the young
Swiss and he spent the winter there at Fort Clark working on
his paintings while his patron made more notes.

The next spring, on May 27, 1834, Bodmer and his patron
arrived back in St. Louis, loaded with paintings, sketches and
specimens. They went on to New York and on July 16 sailed
for Europe, almost exactly two years after they had first
landed in North America.

Karl Bodmer went back to his old haunts, the Barbizon Art Colony in Fontainebleau Forest near Paris. He proceeded to work at finishing the eighty-one pictures which went into the folio *Atlas* accompanying Prince Maximilian's two-volume *North American Journey*. With its publication, Bodmer became recognized as an artist of first importance. He and his art became very popular at Barbizon and he was soon one of the most admired and influential members of this important art group.

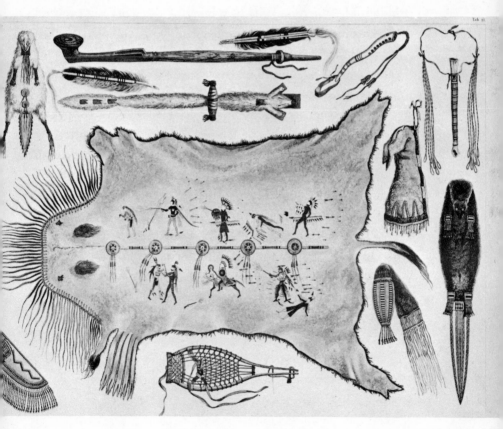

Indian Utensils and Arms *Karl Bodmer*

At the time when Bodmer was enjoying great fame, he befriended a young artist named Jean Francois Millet, a twenty-year-old "poor boy" painter who had his studio in a barn. Later Millet created a sensation with his painting "The Angelus" and other French pastoral scenes.

When Bodmer received a commission from an American publisher to do the illustrations for a work on the colonial wars, he found himself too busy to paint the pictures so he persuaded Millet to paint them from sketches Bodmer himself had made in the United States.

Evidently Bodmer saw no harm in giving the work to Millet. He supervised the beginning of the work, and several of the illustrations (lithographs) had been completed when the publisher got wind of this undercover deal and promptly cancelled the commission. Even so, some of these Bodmer-Millet paintings were reproduced for sale in America.

As time went by, Bodmer's star declined, while the work of his protégé, Millet, became famous and much sought after. At last Bodmer was forced to sell items from the prized collection of Millet's drawings and paintings which he had gathered during the time of their early friendship, including the American Indian lithographs.

Karl Bodmer continued to live at Barbizon until his death on October 30, 1893. He was a perfectionist in several media: acid etching, stone lithography, wood-block engraving, and drawing and painting. He left a peerless representation of the western Indians and their magnificent, unspoiled country.

7

Alfred Jacob Miller, 1810-1874
THE MISTY WAY OF MILLER

ALFRED JACOB MILLER, like many other young artists, began his career by drawing caricatures of his schoolmaster. Most of these first efforts were put into the pot-bellied stove but one of them, "The School Master," dated 1825, is still in existence.

Two years later, when Miller was seventeen years old, he did a drawing that showed such improvement it is believed he may have studied with one of the Peales of the famous Peale Museum in Philadelphia. In the years of 1831 and 1832 the artist did work with Thomas Sully, a noted portraitist of the period, and learned to paint portraits.

Miller, born in Baltimore, Maryland, January 2, 1810, was the son of a grocer, George H. Miller, and Harriet Jacobs Miller. Encouraged by the reputation young Miller built up with his portraits, his parents and friends sent him to France and Italy for study. He arrived in Paris in 1833 and enrolled at The Ecole des Beaux Arts in Paris, one of the finest art schools in the world.

He reported that he was the only non-French student but that he received a warm welcome, and was allowed to attend the Beaux Arts Life School all the time he was in Paris without paying for anything except art materials.

In contrast with the money troubles Catlin had for the greater part of his life, Miller seems to have had few problems of that kind. He had neither wife nor child depending on him and was able to earn enough money for his needs. Later in his life he made a fairly good living from his paintings.

A self-portrait in pencil done on the back of a water color in 1834 shows a rather handsome face with the longish hair and wispy moustache then fashionable among the "Romantic" school of painters in Paris. As he grew older, he wore a pointed beard.

The Romantics, as the clique of art students and painters with whom Miller studied was called, made everything ideal and prettily imaginative. Some of Miller's critics call his Indian figures unrealistic. They say the women are too dainty, the warriors look like Greek heroes, and the horses resemble European steeds.

Miller copied famous paintings in the Louvre and claimed he was the first American artist to be allowed that privilege. After Paris, Miller went to Rome to study. There he copied many noted paintings by European masters. He also did water colors of scenes in Switzerland and made sketches of paintings by other popular artists. Among them was an English water colorist named Joseph Mallord William Turner, who was well-known for the hazy beauty of his landscapes.

Artist Miller admired Turner's work so extravagantly that he wanted to achieve the hazy effect in his own paintings, but he was never able to extract from Turner the secret of the romantic look which distinguished the other artist's work.

In 1834 Alfred Jacob Miller returned to Baltimore. There he rented a studio and placed an advertisement inviting the public to visit his rooms over a music store and examine his

Pierre and the Buffalo   *Alfred Jacob Miller*

copies and sketches of paintings from the finest galleries of
Paris, and from those of Florence and Rome.

Evidently the public did not flock to young Miller's show
of paintings. He illustrated sheet music to pay his rent and in
1837 moved to New Orleans hoping for better luck. He had
only $30 in his pocket, but he located a studio and promptly
painted his landlord's portrait, doing such a good job that he
was able to get other commissions.

It was in New Orleans that Miller met the man responsible
for his western adventure among the Indians.

One day he was painting away on a Baltimore scene (perhaps a little homesick for his home town), when a stranger
walked into the studio and began looking over the pictures
hung on the walls. Miller took him for a military man because
of his erect bearing. He wore a grey suit with a stripe of black,
but no bowie knife showed at the top of his vest as was the
fashion of the day in New Orleans.

The visitor looked over the artist's shoulder at the scene he
was painting, commented that he liked it and left.

In Miller's sketch of a Baltimore scene, the setting sun threw a glow over the city, creating the effect he had often tried for. However, he thought the painting too heavy with detail so he decided to scumble it. To do so he spread a thin film of a mixture of several colors over the distant background and achieved a magical effect — the misty look which became his most noted characteristic. It was Turner's hazy effect, and now he had it!

A few days later the military-looking gentleman came back to Miller's studio and introduced himself as Captain William Drummond Stewart, retired, of the British Army. He told young Miller he was getting ready for his fourth trip to the Rocky Mountain country which he had first visited in 1833, and wanted to take along a competent artist-recorder to sketch the country and its native inhabitants.

Thus Miller met one of the most fabulous characters ever to visit the early West. Captain Stewart, the second son of a rich and titled Scottish family, was considered an eccentric, but in the idiom of the men who knew him as a traveling companion, he was a "rare sport."

When he visited the United States in 1832 he was a retired British officer with a distinguished war record, including service in the Battle of Waterloo. His older brother, who had inherited the family title, two estates (Murthly and Grandtully in Perthshire) and a castle (Murthly), supplied him with additional funds and he set out to travel through western United States and to prove that he was as good a mountain man as ever hunted, trapped and explored the West.

Captain Stewart wanted to record the wonders of the mountains and plains and their Indian owners and take back pictures of them for the walls of his brother's castle in Scotland. His discovery of Alfred Jacob Miller resulted in his commissioning the artist to accompany him on a western trip and paint the rapidly changing panorama which held such fascination for him.

Indians Watching the Caravans *Alfred Jacob Miller*

Soon after this meeting in New Orleans, Miller and his patron went to St. Louis, where Captain Stewart made an arrangement with the American Fur Company for them to go along on the spring overland trip to Fort Laramie and farther west.

The fur company was taking heavy wagons loaded with trade goods to be exchanged for furs. The wagons were closely guarded by an escort of trustworthy young men to protect them on the eight-hundred-mile trail to Laramie through Indian country where every Indian coveted the cargo of guns, knives and colorful gewgaws.

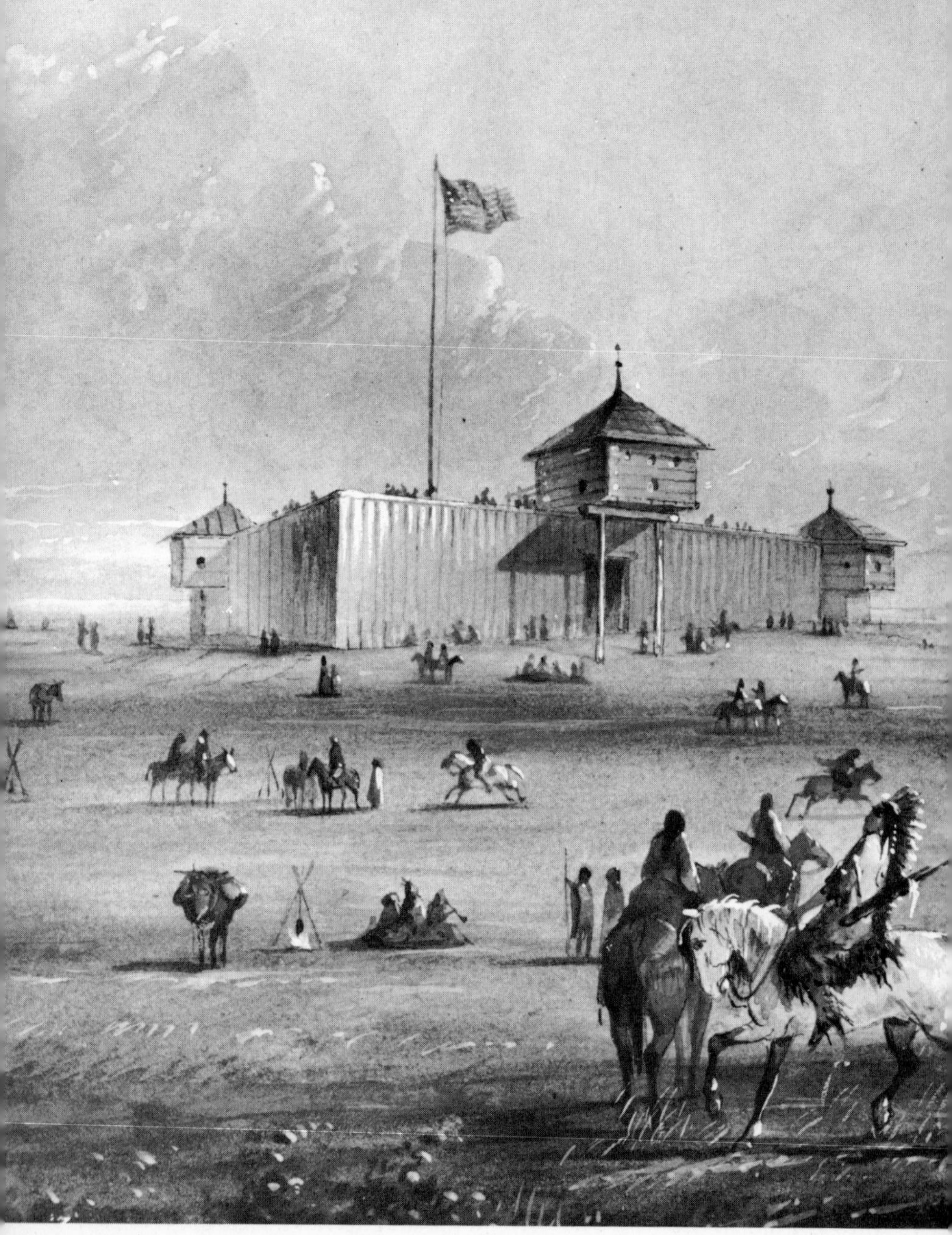

Laramie's Fort *Alfred Jacob Miller*

Miller and the rest of the Stewart party joined the fur caravan at Independence, Missouri, the starting point of the Oregon Trail. At the beginning it was decided that, in view of Stewart's war experience, he would take charge of the caravan if it should be attacked by Indians.

The artist was a complete novice in the ways of the West, and it is said that he showed little interest in the exciting events of his experiences there, but he painted a colorful picture, "Threatened Attack," and other scenes of action which indicate that he was not really indifferent to the drama of men of European background invading the red man's land.

A brief stop at Fort Laramie gave Miller a chance to make a sketch of the fort. Then the wagon train pulled on through South Pass to the Rendezvous in Green River Valley, Wyoming.

Here he and his patron spent a month at the Rendezvous, the big trade meeting and sports festival of the year for the Indians, fur traders, trappers and hunters of the area.

Miller's sketches and paintings of this annual affair were as colorful and exciting as the meeting between the white men and the natives, mostly of the Snake tribe. The Indians had a grand parade especially for the Stewart party — a truly magnificent spectacle which was duly recorded. The other festivities went on through the days and far into the nights: horse races, ball games (Indian style), wrestling and singing and dancing to the music of Indian drums. There was feasting also, provided by the fur company and enjoyed by all.

When the Rendezvous broke up, the Stewart party moved on to New Fork for a campout in the captain's favorite spot.

Miller painted several pictures of this beautiful region and the surrounding country.

Every situation has its drawbacks, and Miller had a problem. Captain Stewart ran his expedition with military precision and discipline from which not even the artist was exempt. Each man had clearly defined duties, such as rounding up his own horse in the morning (they were released early to graze). Miller was often forced to run a long way in his moccasins before he could catch his mount. However, he was allowed to pay someone to take over his guard duty and to put up his tent.

The hunter, Antoine Clement, supposedly a half-breed of Indian and French-Canadian blood, took Miller under his wing and helped him get near enough to the buffalo to sketch them in their various moods and attitudes. Sometimes he made on-the-spot sketches with pen and pencil, or in water color. Others, including wash drawings, were outlined and finished back at camp. Antoine, young and handsome, proved a fine subject and appeared in several pictures.

Campfire – Preparing the Evening Meal   *Alfred Jacob Miller*

Miller made in all something over three hundred pictures during the short time he was in the West, a surprisingly large output. While this did not equal Catlin's prodigious amount of work, Miller's pictures have delighted a great number of people and have added notably to our record of the early West. As to their accuracy, Miller was the only one of the five artists who traveled with a fur brigade. He saw the fur trade when it was at its height. He met so-called wild Indians and the mountain men — Kit Carson, Jim Bridger and others — in person. He attended one of the famous fur Rendezvous. In short, like Kilroy, Miller was there.

Captain Stewart, in spite of his discipline, was a man who enjoyed life and wanted others to have a good time. It is doubtful that he urged the artist to greater efforts as Bodmer was allegedly goaded by his patron, Prince Maximilian, so we assume that Miller savored the pleasures of western life along with the rest of the party.

After leaving New Fork, Stewart's party stopped at Green River camp, then came on to St. Louis. From there Miller hurried back to his New Orleans studio and began the work of making the sketches into finished paintings.

He first exhibited the pictures in his home town of Baltimore in 1838. The local newspapers gave him an enthusiastic write-up. However, one of them printed an article criticizing the mistiness of his landscapes (achieved by scumbling, a la Turner) as untrue to nature's coloring. His pencil sketches were admired by all who saw them as representative of the "Far West."

In May, 1839, just before Captain Stewart returned to Scotland, the Apollo Gallery in New York showed a small collection of Miller's western paintings. Newspaper notices of the New York showing praised the scenes of the Rocky Mountains, the portraits of Crow and Snake Indians, and the sketches of the sports and customs of the natives and the trappers. It was also noted that after ten days they would be shipped to the home of their owner, Captain Stewart, a veteran of seven years of hunting and exploring in the West.

Stewart, on the death of his brother in 1839, became Sir William Drummond Stewart and master of the estates in Scotland. When he left the United States to assume his new responsibilities, he took with him many souvenirs of the West: buffalo grass, redbirds, buffalo, antelope and a grizzly bear, as well as many shrubs and plants.

He persuaded his hunter-companion, Antoine, and two Indians to join him on his estate. Then in 1840 he summoned artist Miller to his home and set him to work making more western sketches into oil paintings for Murthly Castle.

Alfred Jacob Miller spent a year in the ancestral home of Sir William Drummond Stewart, Baronet, Murthly Castle, Scotland. There the artist lived luxuriously, with every comfort provided. He also shared the social life of his patron. This was all very different from the rugged days in the Rockies and the iron discipline Captain Stewart had maintained while in the West.

However, Miller did not devote all his hours to having a good time. He worked on the pictures that Sir William wanted to display on the walls of the castle. He also did a portfolio of water colors which was placed in an elegant binding and shown to important visitors at the castle, bringing many compliments to the artist.

During the winter of 1841-1842 Miller was in London, doing a religious picture for the chapel of his patron, Stewart, who had become a Catholic while in the United States. Miller also visited with Catlin, who was in London at the time, and it is likely that he got from the always needy Catlin the idea of making copies of his western water colors. At any rate, he later turned out many oil and water-color duplicates of his western and Indian pictures originally made in 1837-1838.

Sir William Stewart had one last fling in the land he had enjoyed so much. In the year 1843 he brought a party of guests to the Rockies for a hunting frolic. He housed them in luxurious splendor never before seen in the vicinity: there was a huge red tent, with Persian rugs to carpet the prairie grass, linen sheets on the buffalo-robe beds, and silver toilet articles in the bedrooms. These and other niceties of civilization had been imported for the occasion, and Sir William Stewart's friends hunted, feasted and raced their horses to their heart's content. The Indians in the area entertained with their own show, dancing, yelling and drum-beating in the fire-lighted pattern of century-old ceremonials.

Alfred Jacob Miller went home to Baltimore in April, 1842. Evidently he had seen as much of the world as he cared to see and was ready to settle down to a comfortable existence as artist-in-residence and portrait painter for his home town. While he was doing portraits for the elite, he was also turning out duplicates of his Indian and western sketches for the local westophiles. He painted a number of sketches for Wm. T. Walters at $12 each, complete with short notes, between February, 1859, and August, 1860.

There seems to be no accurate count of the number of water colors he made. It was his favorite and most effective form of art, and his output of originals and duplicates probably ran into several hundred. He had learned the "Romantic" style in Paris, and later added his own version of scumbling, which gave his pictures the magical misty look on which his fame largely rests. But his portrayal of Indian and western scenes offers a faithful record of the magnificent panorama that unfolded before his eyes. He was a "picture writer" of excellence, unsurpassed and unequaled in his field.

8

Frederic Remington, 1861-1909
ATHLETE-ARTIST-AUTHOR

FREDERIC REMINGTON was a late-comer to the Old West, one of the last important artists to see it. He sketched and painted some of the last days of the wild and woolly era. In western art this began with George Catlin's paintings and came to an end with the death of Charles M. Russell.

Remington was born in 1861, the first year of the Civil War, at Canton, New York. He was the son of a distinguished cavalry officer who later became a newspaper publisher.

Young Frederic attended the Military Academy at Worcester, Massachusetts, and afterward entered Yale University as an art student determined to learn about the arts of sketching and painting which had attracted him at the Military Academy.

However, he seems to have been sidetracked at Yale by his deep interest in sports. He was a good football player. With his fine physique, Frederic was able to make the team captained by the famous Walter Camp. In addition, Frederic Remington loved to box. He spent so much time boxing and became so proficient at it that he was rated a near-professional heavyweight.

The Bronco Buster   *Frederic Remington*

There was much literary talent in the Remington family, so Frederic was interested in writing too, but his art study came first. He had a remarkable career in both fields.

While he was very young he read many books and papers of history and adventure, including the Catlin papers, those of Lewis and Clark and Francis Parkman. In this reading he developed a knack for getting at the heart of a story or incident. Whichever medium he was using, he always presented his theme with dramatic force.

Perhaps the fact that his father was a cavalry officer had some bearing on Remington's never tiring of painting and sketching cavalrymen and cavalry horses. With dashing skill, his cavalrymen gallop across the plain, among the rocks and into gulches. With straight backs and high behinds, they dodge Apache arrows with hardly a quiver of the moustache.

In picturing a tragedy of Indian attack or some other disaster, Remington was always a great documentarian with a heart. His pictures appealed to millions of easterners who saw

The Cavalryman   *Frederic Remington*

his sketches in *Century Magazine* in the 1886-to-1888 period. They still have the same strong attraction for his many admirers.

In 1886 the artist received a commission from *Century Magazine* to do documentary pictures of Indians on the reservations and also to write articles about them.

Because there were almost no cameras in the West in the late 1880's, the artists interpreted the news and also illustrated stories and articles in journals and weeklies, painting scenes of vigorous action in the mountains and plains.

Remington in 1881 made a short trip to Montana and evidently found a lot of adventure in that rugged country. On his return from this trip he sold a drawing to *Harper's Weekly*. It was just a forerunner of the many others he would sell to that magazine.

One of Remington's earliest cowboy pictures to be published was "In From the Night Herd." It is thought to be a likeness of the artist himself. This illustration appeared in *Harper's Weekly* of October 8, 1886, when the red-haired painter was still slim but rather husky. In later years he put on considerable flesh, at one time weighing 230 pounds in spite of the strenuous activities of his life.

There is a saying that every man is entitled to make one mistake in his life. Remington made one when he bought a sheep ranch in Kansas. As the Kansans tell it, the story goes like this:

When Remington's father died in 1880, he left his son an inheritance of several thousand dollars. Fred left Yale and began looking about for a way to make a quick fortune which would support him in the free and affluent style to which he thought an artist should be entitled.

A friend, Robert Camp, whom Remington had met at Yale, had gone to Kansas after graduating. Young Camp was sheep-ranching in that state in 1882. He wrote glowing accounts of his life as a sheep-rancher to try to persuade his friend Remington to go into the sheep business, using his inheritance for the investment. Cattle raising, Camp pointed out, was too expensive for a beginner.

Finally, Remington after receiving many enthusiastic letters from his friend, allowed Camp to buy for him, sight unseen, a 160-acre ranch in Butler County adjoining Camp's own place. Butler County was in the Flint Hills where the blue stem grass grew high and handsome — when it grew!

In those days there was no stigma attached to sheep raising and none of the cattle vs. sheep battles portrayed in many western movies had yet developed. Remington and Camp had neighbors, two young bachelors of similar tastes, and the foursome of ranchers were collectively known as "the boys." Sometimes they were called "them young hellions," but for the most part the high-spirited "boys" were well liked by neighboring ranchers.

One of the four was James Chapin, owner of a nearby ranch. The fourth was a Britisher, Charlie, a hearty, hail-fellow-well-met remittance man, the younger son of a prominent English family who received funds from home. Charlie had a horse ranch down the creek and was a sociable fellow. He often rode the seven miles to visit Remington and Camp. Sometimes he came at the inconvenient hour of three in the morning.

Remington's ranch was 160 acres of unfenced land, on which stood a three-room house consisting of a long living-room below, a bedroom above, and a lean-to kitchen on the side.

Robert Camp had gotten a spring clip of several thousand pounds of wool that year, and Fred Remington believed his visions of growing rich in the sheep business had every chance of coming true.

First, he must have horses. All the ranchers had horses to work, to ride and to race. Arguing the good points of their horses and racing them was a popular pastime. Betting was brisk, and the unwary stranger was likely to get well "skunked," as the Butler County folk expressed it.

Remington was lucky enough to get hold of a gold-colored mare with thoroughbred lines which became his favorite mount. He called her Terra Cotta for her unusual coloring and her yellow mane and tail. The ranch hands, not being artists, called her Terry.

He hired a young helper, Bill Kehr, who was also a boon companion. Bill had horses too, notably Prince, a poky-looking old gray plug who was deceptively faster and livelier than he appeared.

Bill Kehr was supposed to look after the sheep while Fred cared for the horses and did the cooking. About his cooking little is known, but the neighbors commented that the pile of empty tomato cans and sardine tins in the Remington yard grew high and wide before the year was out.

As spring came, Remington galloped over the plains on Terra Cotta, enjoying the freedom of the range where buffalo no longer roamed. He lost the rather distant air he had displayed when he first came to Butler County. His artistic sense started to respond as he began taking an interest in his neighbors and their children.

He sketched ranch scenes, the sheep, the horses, the cows and the people of Butler County.

Often on Sunday evenings a group of ranchers would gather at Remington's and talk and argue while he sketched them. Sometimes they put on a boxing match, a popular pastime then, but none of them dared to take on Remington, who was a boxing star and did not hesitate to maul anyone who dared to oppose him in a match. In sports, as in everything he did, Fred Remington gave his all. "Let the best man win," was his motto.

Stampeding the Wagon Train Horses   *Frederic Remington*

Riding and working with his horses kept the artist-athlete in good condition. His fine physique served him well later in the half-wild, rowdy West.

With young Bill Kehr in charge of the sheep, Remington rode horseback into the surrounding country. He went south into Indian Territory (now Oklahoma), southwest into New Mexico, and west to Dodge City, Kansas. Everywhere he found new and exciting subjects for brush and pencil.

Remington wrote friends about his experiences in "running jacks," the over-sized, long-eared rabbits of the plains. After the dog, a greyhound, flushed the jacks out of the brush, the hunters, armed with lances (small poles several feet in length), chased the fleeing jacks and tried to touch them with the poles. It was not as easy as it sounds.

On one occasion, seven men showed up for the sport, including Charlie. The remittance man came attired in the correct hunting togs worn for fox hunting in England — all except the red coat, which he felt was a bit too much for the occasion. It is not recorded if he shouted "Tallyho" at sight of the quarry.

Jack rabbits were plentiful in Kansas at that time and at first sight of one the hunters were off. The rabbit crossed them up by doubling in his tracks and running into a slew. In the excitement of chasing the jack, the riders, galloping pell-mell across the rough ground, lost their seats and wound up sitting on the ground and wondering what had happened. They were bruised and baffled and hadn't hit the rabbit.

Chasing a second jack let them into the yard of a newly arrived rancher. The boys circled to resume the chase, but the rancher, an old man, appeared on the scene and invited them to breakfast. So they declared amnesty on the jacks, licked their lips and accepted the bid, food being more important than sport at that moment.

While the meal was cooking, the hunters looked over the old man's corral and one of them made a kidding remark about the stock it contained. This brought a protest from the old man. He had a little old mare, he said, that could run some. Immediately the boys challenged the rancher to a race: his little old mare against Jim Chapin's mount, Push-Bob, and Prince, the grey plug owned by Bill Kehr. This would not only determine how fast the little mare could run but also would settle the often disputed matter of whether Push-Bob or Prince was the faster for the quarter-mile distance.

As usual the boys wanted to bet on the race. They looked over the old man's mare and decided she looked too old and feeble to make much of a showing, so the betting became fervid between the other two.

The Englishman bet his mare against a three-year-old. Remington staked his beloved Terra Cotta against another mare and her colt, belonging to the old man. Remington's pal, Robert Camp, wagered his mount against four head of the old man's cattle. They set up the finish line on the prairie and let the old man's son and two of the hunters be judges. Remington was to fire the gun to start the race.

The old man, shirtless and with his grey hair tossed by the wind, lined up his mount with professional skill. The two boys, barefoot and with sleeves rolled high and handkerchiefs tied around their heads, pulled up beside the mare and waited for the signal.

When Remington fired the starting shot, the old man on his mare took the lead and stayed in front all the way. Push-Bob and Prince ran neck and neck all the way — behind.

There was weeping and wailing among the boys. Remington lost his beloved Terra Cotta, a loss that almost broke his heart.

As the horseless boys watched the old man put their horses into his corral, leaving them to walk the ten miles back to the ranch, they lost their appetites. When the old man reminded them of the breakfast invitation, they said they didn't feel like eating. They turned toward home with their saddles piled on the back of old Bob, the mule, which one of their gang had ridden in the jack-running.

The bitterest pill to swallow was the thought of the old man telling everybody in the county about how his little old mare outran Prince and Push-Bob and gave him six good horses for his corral.

When Remington and his helper, Bill Kehr, rode on spare horses to the grocery at Plum Grove to purchase supplies, they peered through the front of the store and saw the old slicker sitting on a barrel and entertaining the crowd with an account of the race. It brought a big laugh and the two suckers quietly turned their horses toward home without entering the place. It was better to go hungry or eat potatoes.

One of the things thought responsible for Remington's decision to leave sheep-ranching to others was an occurrence well remembered by the Butler County folk.

The people of Plum Grove and the nearby neighbors from the ranches had gotten up a Christmas party to be held in the schoolhouse.

Remington and the "boys" were in the audience that night. Another resident of the area, one they disliked, was also present and occupying a front seat. The sight of his gleaming bald head was too inviting for the boys to resist and they began pelting it with paper wads and mud balls. This misconduct by the boisterous Remington crowd brought a reprimand and a request to leave.

Once outside, the "boys" spotted a straw-pile. One reckless youth suggested they stack the straw against the windows and set it on fire. That brought the crowd erupting from doors and windows in panic. Luckily, there were no injuries, but much indignation. Warrants were sworn out for the arrest of the "boys" for their unseemly conduct, and the neighborhood had a new subject for their talks.

In District Court the jury disagreed and the case was dismissed on payment of costs. The costs, including fees and other expenses, came from Remington's pocket. He and the "boys" were apparently forgiven. However, the whole affair embarrassed him very much and a short time later he made up his mind to give up ranching.

There was a terrific slump in the market in the spring of 1884 when Remington harvested his first crop of wool, and very likely this was the last straw which made him decide to sell his two quarter-sections of land, his sheep and his horses and leave Kansas after just one year of sheep-ranching.

9

REMINGTON KNEW HORSES

IN THE SHORT TRIP he had taken across Montana before his sheep-ranching days, Remington had an experience which made him realize he must begin his painting and sketching of the Old West before it vanished.

He had stopped at the campfire of an old wagon-freighter who invited the wanderer to share his bacon and coffee. Remington was nineteen years old at the time. As they smoked their after-supper pipes, the old man told how he had come out West when very young and had worked his way farther and farther on with the tide of civilization. He predicted that the end of the old frontiers was in sight and that the railroads would soon come puffing along the Yellowstone River.

This brought the artist up against a fact he had tried to ignore — the old wild life and the open country he loved were about to become a thing of the past.

So Remington began to fill his sketch book with western subjects. There were Indians, cowboys, troopers, old-time cavalry officers, cattle and horses — always horses.

After the sale of his sheep ranch, Fred Remington moved to Kansas City, the big town of the area, and bought a small interest in a saloon. He painted pictures to hang in his place of business, delighting the cattlemen and other customers with his rugged, realistic portrayal of western scenes of battles with nature or of Indians fighting enemy tribes.

On October 1, 1884, Remington married the sweetheart of his boyhood days, Eva Adele Caton. The young couple lived in Kansas City.

However, the course of true love did not run smoothly and they met financial reverses. Remington lost his partnership in the booming saloon business and then began to realize that he could not depend upon selling his sketches and paintings to provide a living for himself and his bride.

Sadly enough, the new Mrs. Remington returned to her father's home. Frederic, again trying to make a lucky strike and get rich quick, went to Arizona to prospect for gold. This venture proved to be a failure, too, and the artist set out on a wandering course which took him through the Apache Indian Reservation. Luckily he ran into a unit of cavalrymen who were overseeing the Apaches, and joined them to share their bunks and scanty rations.

The friendly and likeable Remington was always well received by other men. He was interested in riding, boxing, rifle marksmanship and, of course, in sketching the sandy wastes and canyons and the Indians of the reservation. It seemed that every man of the tribe always had a horse of some sort, and each owner made an effort to decorate his pony in colorful and unusual fashion. The young Indians galloped about with no object in view except to show off the speed and endurance of their mounts. The Apaches were worth painting and the artist gave them plenty of space in his sketchbook.

Eventually Remington got his fill of wandering and began to think seriously of his future. Late in 1885, he arrived in New York City with three dollars in his pocket and a harvest

The Scout *Frederic Remington*

of sketches of western scenes. He was determined to make a new start in the business of illustrating and painting. He persuaded his wife to come to New York and they again took up life together on a slender budget.

A picture previously sold to *Harper's Weekly*, entitled "Roused by a Scout," was redrawn and appeared on February 25, 1882. Another of his western scenes was reworked by another artist and appeared in *Harper's Weekly* on March 25, 1885.

With these small successes under his belt, Remington tried desperately to sell more of his western pictures. He walked

Fired On   *Frederic Remington*

from one New York publishing house to another, and borrowed money for living expenses. He even showed up at classes at the Art Students League but, as before, he failed to get what he wanted from art lessons.

Finally the persistent artist made a sale to *Harper's Weekly* which was published, without being reworked, in the January 9, 1886 issue. That seemed to break the dreary pattern of ill luck. In that same year Remington sold to three different magazines.

Soon his pictures became so popular that editors looked him up — a welcome change from the days when he had walked the streets seeking work. His paintings, "The Courier's Map of the Trail," appeared in the National Academy's exhibition.

Remington was now deeply involved with his art work. He labored early and late and turned out an amazing number of pictures — all portraying scenes of the Old West. In 1890 he sold one hundred and seventy illustrations to leading magazines!

Frederic Remington's meeting with Theodore Roosevelt brought together two men with a single viewpoint — the rugged, outdoor one. Roosevelt admired Fred's work and after the artist illustrated Roosevelt's first book, *Ranch Life and the Hunting Trail*, they got well acquainted and were soon close friends.

One of the things Fred had dreamed of doing was illustrating Longfellow's *The Song of Hiawatha*. This became a reality when he was commissioned to do a series of paintings for that poem. He also illustrated other literary works, including Francis Parkman's *The Oregon Trail*.

Even with a steady income, Remington did not relax into a comfortable existence in his studio. Every summer he went west and lived with the cowboys, the cavalrymen, and the Indians, just as he used to do before he became famous. He rode and ate and slept with the westerners and studied their way of life in detail so that he could reproduce it in true perspective.

Frederic Remington's sculptured pieces, beginning in 1895, are not as widely known as his pictures. However, his statuettes of the West, "The Cowboy," "The Bronco Buster," and others, are considered by many experts to be superior to his paintings.

Illustrating his own articles brought Remington many admirers. Both his writing and art were called documentary but his knowledge of details and his gift for presenting the dramatic in both media led him to fame and fortune. The public loved his articles as much as they did his pictures.

In 1897 he tried his hand at writing fiction. *Harper's* published his *Sun-Down* stories. They were later made into a book, published in 1889. Then came his first novel, *John Ermine of the Yellowstone*, published in 1902. This went into several editions, and was made into a play that was produced in Chicago and New York and played in road shows for a number of seasons. His book, *The Way of An Indian*, appeared serially in *Cosmopolitan Magazine*, November, 1905 to March, 1906. It was published as a book in 1906.

Frederic Remington's list of accomplishments in sculpture, painting and writing is almost unbelievable. In addition to these, he was a world traveler and a war correspondent with the army under General Shafter in the Spanish-American War.

With his work now selling to an appreciative public, Remington was able to move to a fine estate with a studio so large he could have live horses and riders pose for him in it. He was proud of his ability to draw, paint and model horses. He told reporters to write about his work — not about him. "Say, 'He knows horses,' " he urged them.

All kinds of people have admired Remington's work. His pictures are found in museums, art galleries, clubs, private homes — sometimes in old hotels and in bars and saloons. Wherever men congregated to talk sports, business or politics, or just to exchange ideas, Remington was a prime favorite. His painting of "Custer's Last Stand" was reproduced many times. From the Arizona period of his wandering he painted a rouser, "The Apaches Are Coming." His "Indian Scouts on Geronimo's Trail" appeared in *Harper's Weekly* as did "Dismounted," "Arrival of a Courier," "A Friendly Scout Signalling the Main Column," and "Signalling the Main Command." Full of tragic feeling were his sketches "Shot on Picket," and "Burial Party."

In picturing the vanishing cowboy, the bucking bronco, the wild steer on a rampage, the roundup, even the lonely buckaroo singing to the night herd, Remington won the hearts of westophiles and became the most popular artist of his time.

He died after an emergency appendectomy at age 48, December 26, 1909, when his talents were in full flower. Both his pictures and his writing left us an authentic record of the Old West in the transition period between the last quarter of the 1800's and the beginning of the 1900's. It was all presented in Frederic Remington's own inimitable dramatic style.

10

Charles Marion Russell, 1864-1926
ARTIST IN COWBOY BOOTS

When Charles Marion Russell arrived in Helena, Montana, in March, 1880, his first sight of the mining-camp town was bitterly disappointing.

Although it was crowded with Indians racing their ponies down the dusty streets, none of the redskins was wearing a warbonnet and not an arrow zinged past his head. Nor were the whites (miners and mountain men) garbed in fringed buckskin shirts and rawhide pants, as he had seen them pictured in stories of the West. But there was nothing disappointing about the scenery. The snowcapped mountains, the giant trees, the canyons and gulches and grassy plains were just as he had imagined them.

Charlie was a sixteen-year-old greenhorn fresh out of St. Louis, where he had been born March 19, 1864, the third of six children of Charles Silas Russell and Mary Mead Russell. The family estate was in a suburb of St. Louis. There the Russell family dispensed old-fashioned hospitality.

Their comfortable living-room was furnished with life-size portraits of generations of Russells. Among these was a likeness of William Bent of the famous Bent brothers who were associated with the fur trade in the early 1800's. They had spent their lives trading with the Indians and the white trappers.

The Bents were Charlie's great-great uncles, William, Charles, George and Robert. George Bent was with the American Fur Company in 1816. Charles was in the Santa Fe trade. Later, in 1846, he was appointed governor of New Mexico Territory. William Bent, Charlie's hero, built a trading post on the Arkansas River in 1824 and settled there. He was a trusted friend of the Indians in the area and well-known to the hunters and mountain men such as Jim Bridger, Kit Carson, and Bill Williams.

In 1828, William Bent and a relative, Ceran St. Vrain, had started building famous Bent's Fort, fifteen miles below the present Pueblo, Colorado. It had taken them four years to construct a huge adobe fortress, trading post and living place, which was for many years a haven of rest for all travelers on the Santa Fe Trail. It spelled hospitality, and quite often safety from Indian attack.

Probably the influence of the stalwart Bents had a great deal to do with Charlie's desire to go West and see its wonders for himself. Besides, the St. Louis river-front atmosphere — steamers, keelboats and other water craft, the French-Canadian voyageurs, the mountain men, roustabouts and half-breed Indians — all served to fire his imagination. He haunted the wagon yards, the horse and mule lots, and the gun and harness shops where men gathered to plan their excursions into the untamed West.

While in school, Charlie, like the other boys, had read the thrillers — dime magazines and weeklies — that told of the exciting events of the surge into the West. He saw himself in every adventure, living and dying with each heroic character.

Jerk Line   *Charles M. Russell*

The West was more real to him than anything happening in his own life.

Charles M. Russell's artistic talent showed itself early. At the ripe old age of four he was soundly spanked for drawing pictures on the front steps and on the clean fireplace hearths. Even the walls were decorated with youthful drawings of Indians and ponies. Modeling came naturally to him. He used beeswax or any other soft material his small fingers could squeeze into the shape of an eagle or a horse.

His first recorded modeling job was made from a picture of an eagle bearing the inscription, "Copyright Reserved." Charlie's plaque of the eagle also bore the words, although he was too young to read or understand them. He told his mother that was the eagle's name. When he was eight years old he began molding many small animals of wax, using toothpicks for legs and bristles from paintbrushes for tails. These little statuettes were so lifelike that his father bought some beeswax for him to use for more animals. Charlie would lie belly down on the ground or on the floor and shape a magnificent bear, a stately buck or a charging elk, while the talk went on around him. Later in life, he became so proficient that he could model without looking at his work.

Of course, the boy Charlie didn't spend all his time drawing or modeling. He had a pony, a gift from his father. Charlie loved horses and riding, and from that time on always owned a saddle horse.

In Charlie's imagination, the gully near his home was War Whoop Gulch, and the woods surrounding the area were full of wild Indians and ferocious beasts.

The youngsters he played with liked to dress in turkey-feather war bonnets and paint their faces with clay. Then they would steal the dolls belonging to the girls, scalp them and burn them at the stake, as the Indians reportedly treated captives.

Charlie's mother was an artist in her own right who drew
pictures to entertain her son and always had a loving and
sympathetic ear for his problems. In addition to the artistic
talent he inherited from her, Charlie also had his mother's
humor and lighthearted outlook on life. He was as famous
among his friends for his funny stories and jokes as for his
painting and modeling.

Charlie's father was a voracious reader. Every evening when
he went into the library to read, the children would follow
and beg him to read to them. What he read was history: tales
of Daniel Boone, Davy Crockett, and other heroes of hair-
raising adventures. Charlie, lying on the rug with a ball of wax
in his fingers, listened. As he worked, no doubt he planned his
own adventures in the West.

School was an ordeal for Charlie, who could not study for
wanting to be out riding his pony in the woods. In the school-
room he drew animals on the margins of the pages in his books.
They were wonderful animals — which his teachers didn't appreciate. His geography, still in existence, is a treasure-house
of sketches of Indians and cowboys.

Charlie often felt himself too sick to go to school in the
mornings, but after the carriage had taken the other children,
the boy artist would recover quickly. He would spend the
rest of the day roaming the woods on his pony's back, with his
little dog trotting behind. If there was a muddy place around,
Charlie would get off and walk through it until he collected
a goodly supply of mud and clay on his boots. This he would
model into little ponies and dogs.

He would stand these on his desk at school to please the
other pupils. He used to model Indians and small animals with
which to bribe his classmates to do his lessons for him. That
left him free to play hookey down at the water front.

Charlie's chum, Archie Douglas, helped him get away from
the hated routine of school for several weeks. Archie was a

good penman. He wrote a note to the teacher saying that Charlie was going on a long visit to a relative — and it worked.

Every morning during that visit Charlie rode in the carriage with the other children as far as the corner near the school. Then he hid his books and lit out for the river-front or the wagon yards or the mule barns to watch the fascinating panorama of the St. Louis levee — boats loading or unloading, mules being driven from one place to another, fur traders, hunters and trappers landing or embarking on the long journey to the West.

St. Louis was then the world's largest mule market. The mules clattered over cobblestones as they were herded about, bells jangling, drivers yelling and prospective sellers shouting their virtues. Charlie saw himself joining a freighting outfit and drifting West.

In the seventh week of Charlie's truancy he met his father at the corner where he was wont to board the carriage for his return trip home. The elder Russell told his son to go home — he would attend to him later. Charlie knew his father was onto him and decided this was the time to make a break, but when he went back to the mule market hoping to find a place with an outfit bound for the West, the men urged him to go home and stay there until he was big enough to be a muleteer.

At fourteen, Charlie was sent to a military school at Burlington, New Jersey, with the promise that after one year of school he could go West if he wanted to, though his father would have been happier to have the boy enter his own successful brick and clay products business.

At the academy, Charlie "studied" the dime thrillers, hiding them in his books. Sometimes in the midst of a battle with attacking Indians on every side, the teacher would rap the absorbed boy on the head and confiscate the book, leaving Charlie to wonder how it all came out. He told friends that he would never have learned to read if it had not been for the dime thrillers but he spent many hours walking guard with a wooden gun in his hands as punishment for rules infractions.

When midterm came, Charlie went home leaving behind the one hundred hours of guard duty he was supposed to walk. He had a ticket and no one tried to stop him. On arrival at home, Charlie learned that his father wished him to attend art school and also had hired a tutor to help him with his regular studies.

It sounded like an ideal setup and the tutor seems to have been acceptable. There would be no rigid rules, only walks in the woods while absorbing knowledge. However, at the art school, Charlie ran into trouble. His art was not the instructor's idea of art. After three days the boy brought home his materials and announced he was quitting. Charlie didn't want to draw a plaster foot — he already drew horses, mules and Indians from life.

Charles M. Russell was big as a boy and as a man. He was broad shouldered, strong jawed, with the thick neck of a wrestler. In spite of this burly appearance, he was quiet, undemonstrative, and friendly, never afraid to be himself.

He had an awkward kind of grace and wore the things his artist's soul demanded: rings on his fingers, a red sash about his waist (at times), with no comment from his associates. In his grown-up world, dealing with wild game, horses, mules, cattle herds and rough men doing rugged tasks, his associates never questioned his masculinity, and his art was much admired. They thought a man was what he was, even though he looked like a blonde-haired Indian (as the deeply tanned Russell did) and painted pictures.

Just before Charlie's sixteenth birthday in March, 1880, his father divulged the fact that he had made arrangements for Charlie to leave for Montana the very next day. He would

go with a young man named Miller, whose father was a
friend of the elder Russell, and would stay with Miller for a
while. They went by train as far as Red Rock, Montana,
which was the end of the track. Then they traveled by stage
coach to Last Chance Gulch, later Helena, Montana. Finally,
the last two hundred miles was made on horseback, accompanied by a four-horse team and wagon, to a sheep ranch in
the Judith River Valley in central Montana.

On a cold, wet evening in March, 1880, Charlie and his
companion Pike Miller stopped at the Korrell Ranch to spend
the night in Korrell's warm shack before going on to Miller's
place.

While the grownups talked in front of the fireplace, Charlie
unloaded his paint box; brushes, water colors, crayon, and a
ball of beeswax. He painted some horses on the backs of old
envelopes. One picture of a pinto pony caught the fancy of
host Korrell and he asked for a larger one like it.

Charlie proceeded to do an Indian on a pony for his host.
Mr. Korrell nailed it up in the shack, where it hung for many
years. This was the first Russell painting hung in Montana —
a forerunner of hundreds.

The job of herding sheep on the Miller ranch irked Charlie.
He had wanted to be a cowboy. He hadn't figured on herding
sheep.

He made friends everywhere. Even the Indians, the imagi-
nary targets in boyhood days of his quick trigger, became his
friends. He admired their physical prowess, their courage and
the way they lived with nature.

While struggling with the obnoxious sheep, Charlie took
advantage of every chance to visit the ranches nearby. He
would lie on his belly (his favorite position) and sketch or
model while he listened to the oldtimers talk. He could make
tiny pictures of the surrounding scenes he had observed while

Indian Camp   *Charles M. Russell*

riding herd on the sheep. But he never drew or painted a sheep. They just didn't mean the West to him.

Charlie always loved a good horse. He soon got rid of the one he had bought in Helena and purchased two cow ponies. One of these was Monte, a pinto he grew to love and which he rode for more than twenty years. Monte and Charlie were inseparable and well-known characters in the area.

The horse transaction brought on a quarrel with Pike Miller, and Charlie quit the ranch. He saddled Monte and led the mare, packed with his blankets, to Utica stage station to inquire about a job as horse herder. But Miller had been there ahead of him and given them the word about Charlie's habit of drawing or sketching instead of looking after sheep, so Charlie got turned down.

Things looked dark for the penniless young Russell. Ranches were few and far between along the Judith River. Yet the one thing he held to was that he was going to stay in the West, not return to the dull business in St. Louis, as he knew his father hoped he would.

Hungry and disheartened, Charlie set out along the trail. At a campsite, he spread his blankets and sat down to think about the situation. A stranger leading two packhorses came along the river road and stopped to talk. He was Jake Hoover, a noted hunter and pioneer in the area.

After questioning the young camper, Hoover suggested that they eat together, and produced a meal of elk meat from his saddlebags. Food loosened Charlie's tongue. He gave his new acquaintance the full story of his trouble with Miller, and made an understanding friend. Hoover took Charlie home with him to his comfortable ranch nearby and gave him two years of training in hunting, trapping, and the other things he needed to know in order to survive in early Montana.

In those two years with Hoover, whom Charlie called "an all-around mountain man," the artist had a chance to study the plentiful wild game in the area: deer, bear, elk and mountain sheep, and the beaver along the creeks.

Hoover, in spite of the fact that he was a professional skin hunter, had a soft spot for the pet deer and other animals that hung around the salt licks near the cabin. The rule was never to kill an animal at the salt licks or in the park where the cabin sat.

Charlie became a fine marksman but he disliked killing the wild things he loved. Instead, he studied them in their natural habitat and learned for himself the art of putting them on canvas.

Later on in life, when he went out hunting he usually wound up by sketching his intended prey and sneaking quietly away.

Hoover had many friends among the ranchers and fur traders. Whenever company rode up to the cabin, Charlie was all
ears. He learned the habits and the language of the pioneers
and listened to the tales they told — many of which he himself
repeated after he became a man and earned a reputation as a
storyteller.

Hoover was no slouch as a jester. Charlie often recalled one
of his tales. Hoover had been on a prospecting trip and when
he returned to his camp in the evening he discovered that a
silvertip (bear) had been there. When Hoover missed a pair
of gum boots, he declared he kept seeing tracks of gum boots
around but no sign of humans — he allowed that the bear was
wearing his boots!

While Jake Hoover was out on his hunting forays, Charlie
worked around the cabin and kept things going. He had
time to do water-color sketches. He dug mud from a nearby
creek and modeled his favorite animals.

Then he built a kiln in which to fire his statuettes, passing
many happy hours in his studio in the cozy cabin.

In after years when Charlie became tired of too much civilization he would ride out to Jake Hoover's place and stay
for long periods, painting or sketching or just following his
old-time friend in his game hunting. He felt that Hoover was
a good man after whom to pattern his life.

After two years with his friend Hoover, Charlie went to St.
Louis for a visit. He brought back to Montana a young cousin,
but the boy died of mountain fever just two weeks after they
landed in Billings, Montana. Charlie was again stranded, with
only a few cents in his pocket. The weather was cold in early
April, and it was two hundred miles to Hoover's warm cabin,
but Charlie struck out and had gone only about fifteen miles
when he met a cow outfit coming in to pick up some cattle
for two ranches in the Judith Basin.

Charlie was hired to nightwrangle the horses. When that work was completed, Charlie got another job as nightherder of three hundred horses for the Judith roundup. When that was over he was hired by a rancher to night-herd his cattle.

Charlie stuck with this kind of work for eleven years. He became a typical Montana cowboy. He said he sung to the horses and cattle like any other night-herder.

The cowboy's lot in those days was a hard one, and the six-shooters they wore strapped to their legs got plenty of use. Charlie stood on his own feet, with no concessions from any-one to his genius for painting. The cattle were wild and often on the prod — impossible to control when the grass was scarce.

The disastrous winter of 1886-1887 was one never to be forgotten in Montana. Charlie Russell, broke and jobless, holed up on one of the ranches where he had worked and painted one of his most widely-known pictures.

It is called "Waiting for a Chinook," and shows an emaciated longhorn standing in the snow with wolves circling around waiting for the half-starved beast to go down.

The Chinook, a warming wind, did not come to melt the icy glaze which covered the two-foot-deep snow, and thousands of cattle died during the eight-weeks duration of that freeze. Some of the cattlemen lost their entire herds.

Charlie's little water color (also known as "The Last of 5000,") which he painted on a bunkhouse table by lamplight made him world famous, but he didn't consider it a serious effort.

The story of how he drew it is:

His friend Phelps, owner of the ranch, was at the table with him and remarked that he'd had a letter from a cattleman who lived at Helena asking about the shape the cattle were in. The boss said he would write his friend and tell him about the dead carcasses strewn over the whole country. Charlie volun-

Fireboat *Charles M. Russell*

teered to send a picture along with the letter. When Phelps
saw the sketch, he said the man wouldn't need any letter; the
little postcard-sized sketch told the whole sad story.

It was a tearjerker that reminded Montana stock men of the
bitter winter and the aftermath when a man could walk for
miles on the bodies of dead cattle without setting foot on the
ground. They had drifted there and just stood waiting for
death.

The horses fared better. They would paw through and find
grass under the frozen crust of ice but the cows would not or
could not rustle for forage. They just humped up and died
by the thousands. After that tragic experience, many of the
stockmen sold their holdings and went out of business. Those
remaining made some arrangements to care for their cattle in
emergencies.

Of Montana's seven tribes of Indians, the ones Charlie knew
best were the Flathead, Arapaho, Kootenai, Blackfoot and
Crow tribes.

In 1888, Charlie and two cowboy friends took a jaunt into Alberta, Canada. One of the three was offered a job as foreman on a ranch and became a permanent resident. The other cowboy soon went back to the United States, but Charlie moved into the tents of the Bloods, a branch of the Blackfeet, and lived as an Indian for a period of six months. While living there he learned the sign language by which all tribes talked to each other. Charlie was a graceful and moving talker in this wild rhythm of the fingers and often used it in communicating with the Indians.

Charlie's stay among the Bloods gave him a chance to learn the details of customs, language, facial characteristics and other traits of the tribe. He always dug for fine points which, once learned, were never forgotten.

The Bloods called Charlie "picture writer." To them he was good medicine. His friend, the chief of the tribe, once asked the artist what the name "Charles" meant, since all Indian names had significance. Russell replied that he didn't know. Then the chief asked what "Russell" meant. Charlie didn't know that either. Thereupon the chief grunted and said he couldn't understand why a white man who was smart and knew paper talk didn't know his own name.

One of Charlie's Indian friends was Young Boy, a Cree, whose brother was a chief. Sometimes Young Boy would walk into Charlie's studio and sit quietly watching the artist work. Then he would ask for a loan, adding that he would pay it back in a certain length of time. After he had the money he would vanish, but he always came back to repay it on time. Young Boy was a frequent subject for Charlie's brush.

Besides the enjoyment his Indian friends gave him, the artist also got material from them for his statuettes and pictures as well as help in collecting Indian costumes and authentic and unusual ornaments. He always attended their ceremonials and festivals, mingling with them and observing their dances.

For Charlie and his white friends, the tribes set up a special lodge of poles covered with hides.

Only an artist with the West in his heart could have obtained from the old men of the tribes the war tales of their youth and the stories their grandfathers had told them. Among Russell's masterpieces of Indian life are "Medicine Man," "Smoke Talk," "Wolf Men," and "Return of the Warriors."

His largest oil painting is "Lewis and Clark at Ross' Hole," a mural twenty-six feet long and twelve feet high now hanging in the Montana House of Representatives. It depicts the historic meeting of the two early explorers and the Ootlashoot Indians at a watering place in the Bitter Root Valley of Montana, and is considered his finest painting.

11

THE LAST PICTURE WRITER

When Charlie ended his stay with the Bloods, he was broke. This was his chronic condition, but now his clothes were ragged and too thin for the weather. His boots, the pride of a cowboy's heart, had worn out and been replaced with moccasins. In this dilapidated condition he started back to his old stamping ground in the Judith Basin.

Charlie managed — as he usually did. A friend provided a new pair of boots for him and money to get to Great Falls. There other friends outfitted him for a trip to Hoover's Ranch. He spent the winter of 1889 on the ranch with his old friend and mentor and painted the scenery in all its grandeur.

The artist was restless at times even in his West. In 1891 he went to Lewiston, Montana, met an old friend and moved into a bachelor shack with him. Although Charlie was broke as usual, he kept painting. He would sell a picture for a few dollars and spend the money for food and liquor for his friends and himself.

One day he was hired to do a picture on the door of a bank vault. He began work at ten in the morning and finished at four in the afternoon. This picture of a cowboy on horseback herding his grazing charges brought twenty-five dollars. Charlie thrust the money in his pocket and started to the store to buy the clothes he needed so badly. But before he could spend the money, he met an old cowhand who was broke and hungry. Charlie's friend had been promised a job but he lacked the money to buy boots. (A cowboy without boots was unthinkable.) Charlie loaned him fifteen dollars needed to buy the boots. Then, when he found that the old puncher was also flat broke, he handed over the other ten dollars.

The artist knew he could always sell a painting for eating money. Besides, as he put it, spring would soon be coming.

Aside from the pictures and statuettes which Charlie was able to sell for a few dollars, he painted for his own amusement and gave his priceless art to his friends. Giving made him happy and he never stopped to consider the value of his gifts.

Friends often urged him to quit the range and be a full-time painter, but Charlie loved the free air of the open range and the rugged life had no terrors for him.

His pictures were hung in saloons, the popular meeting places for all the men of the area. The bartenders often acted as agents in selling Charlie's art to customers: bankers, stockmen, merchants or salesmen. Even the cowboys paid a few hard-earned dollars for his pictures.

Inevitably, the word got around about the cowboy artist. Charlie was in Chinook, one hundred and twenty-five miles from Great Falls, when he got a letter from a bartender named Green enclosing an advance and offering him seventy-five dollars a month and meals if he would come to Great Falls.

It was September, 1891, and prospects for a winter job were poor, so Charlie and a friend packed their gear and set out for Great Falls. Next morning Charlie hunted up the man who

had made the magnificent offer of seventy-five dollars a month
and meals and found there was a catch in the offer. The man
Green pulled out a contract which would have bound the
artist to paint a fixed number of hours every day and turn all
his work over to the contractor.

Charlie always shied away from harness. Signing contracts
was against his nature. He figured that painting was a little different from sawing wood, so he returned the advance money
and decided to try painting for a living on his own.

That winter in Great Falls, Charlie lived with a bunch of
cowpunchers and other men out of work, with their saddles
in pawn and little if anything to contribute to the food pot.
Charlie was the one who kept them eating. He would do a
painting any time a prospective buyer with a few dollars
showed up. It was tough going but they wintered it, and with
the coming of spring in 1892 the punchers all took off for the
cow country. Charlie got lonesome with the others gone, and
went back to his old job of night-herder for what proved to
be his last job on the range.

Charlie and his pals spent the following winter in a shack
in the little town of Chinook. Charlie painted and one of the
gang acted as salesman for the pictures and statuettes he turned
out. The men were full of deviltry and rough humor and
Charlie himself had a full share in it. With spring there came a
great longing for the open range, but this time Charlie was
able to resist it. He was a painter and he meant to stay with it.

He divided his time between Great Falls and Cascade, a cow
town only twenty-five miles away. He painted many pictures
between 1893 and 1896. Most of them were given to friends
but some were sold to the citizens of the towns and others
who had heard of Charlie.

In 1895 Charlie's mother died in St. Louis. The passing of
his beloved mother was a sad blow to Charlie.

The Thoroughman's Home on the Range   *Charles M. Russell*

Something else happened which had a profound effect on
his future. He met a lovely seventeen-year-old girl at the
home of friends, and plop — it happened. He fell in love.
Charlie was wearing his usual artistic getup which seemed
just right for him but which no other cowboy ever wore:
high-heeled riding boots, snug-fitting pants, a bright French-
half-breed sash low around his waist with the ends tucked
into his pocket, and a necktie hanging loose over his grey
shirt. Charlie had expected to spend his life as a bachelor, but
when Miss Nancy Cooper decided she liked this cowboy-
artist more than any other man she had ever seen, he broke
down and told her about his life of carefree roaming and the

rough ways he had followed in the past, and asked her to throw in with him.

So the thirty-two-year-old artist and the lovely young Miss Cooper were married on September 9, 1896. The wedding guest list consisted of nine persons and the honeymoon trip was a walk of a few yards to the one-room shack Charlie had remodeled at a cost of seventy-five dollars.

With the artist's marriage, the old order passed. He realized that now he had responsibilities and began to change his painting methods. His style remained the same throughout his life, but he started to plan and execute his work more carefully. He did larger and more ambitious canvases.

The new Mrs. Russell made some changes in her husband's social life, also. At first it was hard for Charlie to grasp the fact that the old days of painting when he felt like painting and selling his work for a few dollars to feed his friends were no more. Nancy Russell had a good conception of the worth of his pictures and encouraged him to ask more money for them. She impressed him with the idea that instead of there being one pocketbook for all of Charlie's cowpuncher friends, the welfare of the Russells must come first.

That didn't keep Charlie from emptying his pockets for any one of his penniless friends, but he let Nancy carry the pocketbook.

The West was changing, too. The railroads were coming in with settlers. The Indians were being pushed onto reservations and the buffalo had vanished. There were even wire fences to bedevil the cattlemen.

Since Charlie had spent his formative years on the range and with free-hearted cowmen, he had little knowledge of business affairs. Nancy Russell, sensing that her genius husband lacked the ability to hang onto enough money to support them, took over the family finances.

The young lady studied copyright laws and other legal matters so that she was able to manage any of the deals Charlie made for his pictures. He painted, and she sold and handled the money. Charlie never seemed to worry about what happened to his pictures after he had finished them. Painting was his part of the bargain. Charlie did not break off with his old friends but he did climb on the water wagon and stay there, not only on account of his health but in deference to his wife's wishes.

Under Nancy Russell's management, Russell paintings went up and up in price, from twenty-five dollars to a hundred, then on into the thousands.

Charles Russell called his wife his pardner and said that if it hadn't been for her management he wouldn't have had a roof over his head. Never again did he paint a picture and trade it in The Silver Dollar Saloon or The Mint for drinks for the crowd.

When in 1897 the Russells moved from Cascade to Great Falls intending to make it their permanent home, Charlie did not like the house they rented because of its poor lighting. When his father came to visit them, the elder Russell, now proud of his artist son, bought some lots of land and had a home built for them.

This new home was fine for living but a bit too fancy for painting. Charlie yearned for a studio built of logs like the cabin where he had lived with Jake Hoover. In 1903, Charlie had his log studio, with a fireplace at one end of the long room. There he worked on his pictures surrounded by his Indian relics and the cowboy paraphernalia of his days on the range. The furniture of the old log studio was, and is today, rough handmade chairs, tables and benches, all showing hard usage.

A buffalo skull (Charlie's trademark) that he had picked

up on the range had a prominent place among the many articles he treasured. The floor coverings were bear and wolf hides. There were no feminine touches in Charlie's studio; men congregated there to talk and listen and to watch Charlie paint. Sometimes he cooked for his friends at the open fireplace — man food, consisting of beans and bacon or game, with biscuits and coffee, always winding up with dried apples.

Charlie would get up early and work in his studio until noon, while Nancy Russell looked after their rapidly developing business interests.

When summer came, they went to Glacier National Park, a former hunting ground of the Indians. Bordering on Canada, this section had a great variety of wild game: moose, deer, bear and other smaller animals. Here Charlie had his models live and in profusion. He loved this part of the Rockies. He built a summer cabin there on the shore of a lake and made it his mountain studio.

He would work mornings, following the trails with his sketchbook or sitting on his porch watching the mountains and sky. In the evening he entertained his guests, old friends of his cowboy days or eastern artists he was introducing to his mountain retreat.

Charlie and his father had grown closer after the death of Charlie's mother. The elder Russell tried to publicize Charlie's work and made arrangements to enter some of it in the St. Louis World's Fair of 1903. He was highly pleased when Charlie's Indian painting, "Pirates of the Plains," was exhibited.

Charlie's first effort to win honors and cash in the big city was in the fall of 1903 when the Russells went to New York with a bundle of paintings, hung them in a back alley studio and waited for customers.

Charlie was still the reluctant salesman but Nancy showed the pictures to magazine and other publishers while the artist visited with two illustrators he had met in Great Falls. Charlie got to know other artists through his friends and learned some of the technical tricks which had been missing in his earlier works, but there was no great financial gain from the trip. Nevertheless, they went back home in 1904 with Charlie sporting an overcoat of the latest New York style.

Charlie and Will Rogers met and became friends while the artist was in New York. At that time, Rogers was just starting his career as a cowboy humorist who chewed gum and did roping stunts with a lariat. Rogers always said that Charlie was the only western painter whose every detail was where it should be and not even the punchers could find fault.

After the first visit to New York, Charlie and his wife often went on trips there to attend to matters of exhibits and other business with the publishing houses, but Charlie was always glad to get home again.

His big break came in 1911 when he exhibited twenty-five of his finest paintings in New York under the caption "The West That Has Passed." Before this he had been spoken of almost solely as an illustrator of western scenes, but this one-man show of his paintings put him in the foremost ranks of western art.

Charlie had one peculiarity. He never asked anyone how he liked a certain picture. When questioned as to what his masterpiece was, Charlie always replied that he hadn't painted it yet. He was most concerned about what his old-time Indian and cowpuncher friends thought of his pictures.

After the 1911 exhibition, Charles Russell was invited to show his work in the large cities of the United States and also in Canada. These showings, supervised by Nancy Russell while Charlie visited with the Indians and cowboys, convinced all who saw the pictures that Russell was more than a regional artist of the West.

Charlie and Nancy went to London for an exhibition of his

pictures; then to Paris for a show. Charlie was seasick. A rolling ship was different from the back of a bucking bronco. Charlie said there was only one place he wanted to see — home.

Modeling was Charlie's pastime and he was born with the gift.

The ball of clay or beeswax which he always carried in his pocket would suddenly become a little animal without his looking at it. Friends figured he had made thousands of these small figures to give to others but only a few have been set in bronze and preserved, the first in 1904.

His few larger bronzes, notably "When Sioux and Black-feet Meet," "Bronc Twister," and "Bucker and Buckaroo,"

are preeminent in western sculpture. Horses, Indians, cowboys, all came alive under Charlie's gifted fingers.

As the price tag on Charlie's paintings and statuettes soared, he met new people and made new friends. Persons of world-wide reputation came to his little studio in Great Falls, Montana, and passed the word along about his work.

The artist traded jokes and stories with Theodore Roosevelt, Will Rogers and Emerson Hough as well as others of the group of western writers. Movie stars Tom Mix, Harry Carey and Bill Hart visited the cowboy artist. Mix spent fabulous sums for his pictures. And, of course, the old-time punchers and the Indians continued to drop in on him.

Jake Hoover died in 1924 after discovering several rich gold mines in Montana from which he profited little. He prospected in Alaska and was planning to return to Montana to go over some remembered leads when he passed away. But his part in helping young Charlie Russell find himself will never be forgotten.

Next to his wife and his long-time friends, Charles Russell loved his horses. Monte, the pinto he had acquired in his first year in Montana, carried Charlie through his cowboy days, to Canada on his stay with the Bloods and on the trips to find work. The durable Monte lived to be thirty-one years old (a very long life for a horse), spending his old age in comfort in Charlie's corral. During the hard times when the cowboy-artist was forced to pawn his saddle and sell his boots in order to eat, he never even considered parting with his faithful friend Monte.

In 1916 the Russells became the parents of a son — an adopted one. Charlie loved him as if he were his own.

The University of Montana on June 15, 1925, conferred the degree of Doctor of Laws upon Charles Marion Russell for the long and faithful service he had given in portraying and preserving the look and flavor of pioneer days.

Russell died in Great Falls on October 24, 1926. He had said he wanted to be taken to the burial ground in a horse-drawn vehicle since he had no love for automobiles. So an ancient hearse was brought out of storage for him and two black horses drew it to the funeral service. At the church, twenty of Charlie's paintings were hung on the walls of the chancel. In the procession, three saddle horses followed the hearse. Two of them had riders, cowboy friends of Charlie's; the other horse bore Charlie's saddle, with his lariat, gun in holster and his spurs.

CONCLUSION

THE HISTORY OF THESE five artists of the Old West parallels the relationship of other artists and observers of our western scene from early in the last century to the present.

Catlin, despite his American birth and his painting of himself hunting buffalo, was, like Bodmer, essentially a European observer rather than a participant in the themes he painted. Bodmer, who was employed to depict scientific findings of Prince Maximilian, was far removed from the life of America and returned to France for good as soon as his job was over.

Alfred Jacob Miller's self-conscious search for the misty effect of Turner shows his ties to Europe, but he also painted the Old West realistically. He might be said to represent a transitional period between the European approach and the much more down-to-earth American outlook and painting styles of Remington and Russell.

With Remington, we find an artist who lived the life he expressed in his paintings and in his fine bronzes. However, even he did not identify as closely with the West he portrayed as did Charles M. Russell, who literally became his subject matter. Even though Charlie's astute wife finally led him to Europe for the successful exploitation of his work, it was the ranchmen, the trappers and the cowboys of his own West whose company he most valued and whose praise he coveted.

Less than a century elapsed between Catlin's first trip into the wilds of the Upper Missouri in 1832 and the passing of the cowboy artist, Charles M. Russell, in 1926. Yet in that time the wild Old West was born, rose to its tumultuous crescendo, and died.

These five early artists left a faithful and enduring record of its greatness.

BIBLIOGRAPHY

Adams, Ramon and Britzman, Homer *Charles M. Russell*
  Trail's End Publishing Company, Pasadena, California, 1948
Beebe, Lucius and Clegg, Charles *The American West*
  E. P. Dutton & Company, New York, N.Y., 1955
Catlin, George (Edited by Mary Gay Humphries) *Boy's Catlin*
  Chas. Scribner's Sons, New York, N.Y., 1909
DeVoto, Bernard *Across The Wide Missouri*
  Houghton-Mifflin Co., Boston, Mass., 1946
McCracken, Harold *George Catlin and the Old Frontier*
  Dial Press, New York, N.Y., 1959
McCracken, Harold *Portrait of the Old West*
  McGraw-Hill Book Co., New York, N.Y., 1952
Monaghan, Jay (Editor-in-chief) *The Book of the American West* Julian Messner, Inc., New York, N.Y., 1963
Remington, Frederic (Edited by Harold McCracken) *Frederic Remington's Own West* Dial Press, New York, N.Y., 1960
Ross, Marvin C. *The West of Alfred Jacob Miller*
  The University of Oklahoma Press, Norman, Okla., 1951
Russell, Charles Marion *Trails Plowed Under*
  Garden City-Doubleday, New York, N.Y., 1927
Russell Memorial Committee of Great Falls, Montana *The Log Cabin Studio of C. M. Russell* Great Falls, Montana, 1955
Smithsonian Institution (Bulletin-Annual Report) *George Catlin Collection of Paintings*
  United States National Museum, Washington, D.C., 1955
Taft, Robert *Artists and Illustrators of the Old West*
  Chas. Scribner's Sons, New York, N.Y., 1953

INDEX

125